BEYOND
BIRKIE
FEVER

First American Paperback Edition

This is a work of non-fiction. The publisher does not have any control and does not assume responsibility for author or third-party Web sites or their content.

Cover art by Cara-Jo O'Connell. Contact Cara-Jo by email at cara@cara-jo.com or visit her Web site at http://www.cara-jo.com.

Visit Walter Rhein at his author Web site http://walterrhein.blogspot.com/.

DEDICATION

To my wife Zulma, my daughter Sofia and my friends and family who have made cross-country skiing such a joy throughout the years.

To the aid station workers at the Birkie and every other endurance event throughout the world—thank you for your time, you have literally saved my life on more than one occasion!

To the spectators who brave the cold every year and arrive in droves in order to cheer us in.

To anyone who has ever finished the Birkie or dreamed of it.

ACKNOWLEDGMENTS

I would like to sincerely thank Cara-Jo O'Connell for her tremendous job on the cover art for this book. Cara is originally from the Twin Cities and currently resides in Colorado.

Make sure you check out her portfolio at: www.cara-jo.com.

Contact Cara-Jo at: cara@cara-jo.com!

BEYOND BIRKIE FEVER

BY WALTER RHEIN

WHAT IS BIRKIE FEVER?

Cross-country country skiers are hearty folk. The compulsion to race marathon-length distances in sub-freezing conditions requires an eternally optimistic and fiercely independent spirit. The fear of blinding snow or paralyzing cold does not deter them and it has been said that skiers do not merely laugh at adversity, they are completely oblivious to its existence!

America's greatest cross-country ski race is the American Birkebeiner, or "Birkie." Every year, thousands of people journey from all over the globe to Hayward, Wisconsin, for a world-class celebration of life, winter and the competitive spirit.

Before the race, local participants find themselves in the throes of a unique and natural euphoria. They thrill at the prospect of participating shoulder-to-shoulder with elite international competitors in a race through the great Northwoods wilderness. It is the common person's Olympic ideal—Birkie Fever!

Far more than just a severe case of pre-race jitters,

Birkie Fever is an adventurous compulsion that fuses with your very essence and forms an integral part of your innermost being. It is the catalyst for a fundamental joy of life that gives you the courage to expand your dreams and the strength to achieve them.

Beyond Birkie Fever is the story of how America's magnificent cross-country ski marathon can expand your horizons and be the gateway to experiences beyond anything you'd ever hoped to imagine.

THE FIRST BIRKIE AS TOLD BY FOUNDER DAVID LANDGRAF

The American Birkebeiner is the largest cross-country ski race in North America. It is a prestigious, world-class event that is as well run and well loved as any endurance race on the face of the Earth. Every year, skiers come from across the globe to complete their own fifty-kilometer journey from Cable, Wisconsin, to the finish line in downtown Hayward. The glorious course is a veritable cross-country highway that winds through the magnificent Wisconsin Northwoods, offering both beautiful scenery and a challenging physical test. Those who have come to Hayward on Birkie weekend, either as spectators or competitors, know the American Birkebeiner is a unique and special event that has the ability to change your life forever.

Today, the two thousand-plus residents of Hayward are overtaken on Birkie weekend by the influx of skiers. News crews line the streets and the highway that cuts through the center of town is shut down to allow Birkie participants access to the finish line. Late February generally offers mild winter temperatures and if the thermometer hangs near freezing or above, the party can extend long into the night. Finishers gather to cheer in other participants, guzzle a few beers and exchange exuberant stories of their recently completed race.

It's a Northern Wisconsin Mardi Gras!

But that wasn't always the case.

Back in 1973, the American Birkebeiner was just the dream of legendary Northwoods Wisconsin promoter Tony Wise. The first race had less than forty participants and was a considerably different experience than the tremendous spectacle it has become today.

Among those competing in the first event was David Landgraf. Landgraf is something of a living legend, although he's too modest to describe or even think of himself as such. Today, retired and having completed every single Birkie, Landgraf is still competitive with the fastest skiers in the event.

I sat down with Landgraf on December 31, 2010, to get his account of the first Birkie. Initially, I had asked him to write it down himself, but I soon found that when there's snow on the ground, it's fairly difficult to pry the man off the ski trails.

As we enjoyed a bowl of split-pea soup, I took in a lifetime of Birkie photos and mementos displayed on the walls of David's home. It was obvious how elevated a position the Birkie occupied in Landgraf's life and what a fundamental influence the event had been on him. I soon discovered he was a wealth of information on all things skiing as he regaled me with stories about the improvements in equipment and clothing throughout the years as well as the histories of each Birkie.

"That's the year that Adidas introduced a boot that everybody had to have since the only other alternative left your feet feeling like blocks of ice," he said, gesturing at one photo.

"That's the first year that Fischer introduced a ski specifically designed for skating—note how it still had the long, classical tips," he said while gesturing at another.

"That's the year that everybody wore black-and-yellow ski suits because the Norwegians had worn a similar suit when they came for the Birkie the year before."

Many of the developments along the line struck a chord with me. My mom had been a Birkie participant for as long as I can remember, and I have distinct memories of the ripples of excitement that passed through our household from any little advancement in cross-country skiing equipment. Some of the skis, bindings, and boots that Landgraf alluded to were familiar to me, but the others were new and it was satisfying to have somebody fill in the gaps in my knowledge. It's pretty remarkable to consider that within our lifetime, people were still using skis with three-hole bindings on a consistent basis. What's even more remarkable is how much better the technology has become.

As we finished our soup, I hit the voice recorder function on my BlackBerry and pushed the device in front of Landgraf as he jostled with some notes he'd jotted down in preparation.

"I wanted to set the stage as to what 1973 was like," he said and proceeded to list a series of interesting facts: "A gallon of gas was forty cents, the average income was $12,900, and a new house cost you $32,500. The popular films of the day were *The Exorcist, Deliverance, American Graffiti*, and the best picture that year went to *The Godfather*. On the radio you were listening to *Dark Side of the Moon* as well as groups like Led Zeppelin, The Eagles and Abba. But perhaps most importantly, the first American Birkebeiner took place in Hayward, Wisconsin."

At this, Landgraf pushed aside his notes and became reflective. I got the impression he had told this story many times, although I didn't get the sense that he had inflated or exaggerated the tale through repetition. There are some moments in life that are so precious that people seem to do everything they can to preserve their veracity and that's how I perceived Landgraf felt about his first Birkie experience.

It all started with a phone call from Landgraf's childhood friend and fellow founder Ernie St. Germain in early February 1973.

"David," St. Germain said, "Tony Wise is having a cross-country ski race up in Telemark. I dare you to do it!"

Among other things, Wise had established the Telemark lodge in Hayward as well as the Lumberjack World Championships that still are held annually in Hayward to this day. Landgraf had worked at Telemark throughout high school and college, so he was well aware of who Tony Wise was. What he didn't know anything about, at the time, was cross-country skiing.

"A cross-country ski race," Landgraf replied. "What's that?"

"Well you strap some skis on and ski from Hayward to Cable," St. Germain replied.

"Well, that sounds kind of crazy."

"Come on let's do it!"

At this point, Landgraf emphasized that neither he nor St. Germain had ever participated in any kind of endurance sport before. His love was baseball with the occasional game of pick-up basketball thrown in. He had downhill-skied a dozen times or so because he had worked at Telemark and could downhill for free at night, but he had never cross-country skied before. In fact, he didn't even know what a cross-country ski was and neither did St. Germain. But St. Germain, perhaps trusting Wise's ability to create special events, said that since Tony was having this race they should do it and Landgraf eventually agreed.

Thus committed, Landgraf went about the task of getting himself some cross-country skis. He was living in Bloomington, Minnesota, and he went to the local ski shops on a quest for skis, boots, and poles that he could rent for a couple weeks. Eventually finding a pair, Landgraf was beset by another problem.

There wasn't any snow!

No place to practice.

Nothing upon which to train!

After another exhaustive search, Landgraf discovered that although there weren't any ski trails available, there was a large snowbank that surrounded Met Stadium, where the Twins and Vikings played. Presumably, the snow pile was what had been left over after the parking lots had been cleared. Well, Met Stadium was near where Landgraf lived, so he walked over a couple times and skied on top of the big snowbank that surrounded the stadium and after a while figured, "Well, that's not too bad." But he'd never been on a hill, never been on a trail, and those meager laps around the Met comprised the entirety of his preparation.

Today, people train all year in order to have the fitness necessary to complete the Birkie. Fifty kilometers is more than thirty miles! A running marathon is a grueling 26.2 miles and those are generally run when there isn't any snow on the ground. Landgraf had sentenced himself to a distance longer than a marathon in the sub-freezing conditions of a Wisconsin winter, to boot.

He had done no running.

No endurance training.

No bicycle riding—in fact, Landgraf didn't even own a bike.

He didn't even have a decent familiarity with how to balance on a pair of cross-country skis.

This was Landgraf's preparation for one of the most grueling sporting events in North America.

He's the first to admit he simply didn't have the first clue about endurance sports.

But things were about to change.

When you're twenty-three, you can get away with such unprepared craziness.

On the day of the race, Landgraf showed up with his rented equipment at the designated starting area behind Historyland—another Tony Wise creation—in Hayward. Landgraf was wearing a pair of sweatpants, an old wool sweater, cotton long underwear and, appropriately, a tassel hat.

Fewer than forty people were at the start that day.

Somebody shot a starter's pistol.

And off they went ...

Today, the Birkie trail is a national treasure that cuts through the rolling Wisconsin wilderness and is as wide as a county highway. The trail is groomed with the best equipment money can buy and is widely known as one of the premier cross-country ski destinations in North America.

In 1973, that wasn't the case.

Heading across Lake Hayward, Landgraf soon found himself on an unmarked, haphazard trail that wound along on old logging roads and abandoned rail beds. The trail itself had been made by a guy on skis being pulled along behind a snowmobile, which probably an exhausting task to complete in its own right.

For the vast majority of the race, Landgraf never saw another person.

Surely, the fact that *Deliverance* was in theaters at the time did little to abate his concerns.

Slowly, slipping and sliding along on his rented skis, Landgraf made his way toward Cable. Most of the time he was uncertain if he was in the right place. The single aid station reassured him he was still on track, but otherwise he was sure he was lost the entire time.

The one saving grace was that the temperature wasn't all that bad during the first Birkie. Although, as Landgraf recounted this, he was quick to add, "The next year, however, was a brutal fourteen below zero! This was made worse by the fact that we didn't have the right clothing, of course. But that first year wasn't bad."

Hours passed, disappearing into that vortex of time that only exists in the midst of a cross-country ski race, and a despair began to creep in. Cross-country skiing is essentially the act of skiing uphill, which can be fairly tricky on a piece of equipment that is designed to be free of resistance and is made to glide across the snow. Skiing uphill can be difficult even if you know what you're doing, but for somebody who has no idea, it's virtually impossible.

As the kilometers clicked by and the exhaustion set in, Landgraf resorted to crawling up the hills on his hands and knees. His only salvation was that he knew the terrain surrounding Telemark and the finish line was quite a bit more hilly, so as things got more difficult, he knew he must be approaching the end. He perked up when he thought he began to hear the downhill ski lift equipment up at Telemark echoing in the distance.

The hills continued, up and down, and Landgraf trudged wearily on, crawling miserably along. Suddenly, at the top of the next rise, Landgraf caught a glimpse of something that gave him a surge of energy.

There, also beaten, broken and down on all fours, was none other than his old friend Ernie St. Germain.

"The guy who got me into this mess."

Encouraged by the fact that St. Germain looked just as wretched as Landgraf felt, he got inspired and made a super-human effort to catch up.

Flailing like mad, Landgraf eventually pulled up alongside St. Germain at the top of the bunny hill at the Telemark lodge. Some choice words were probably spoken, which have since been lost to history, and the two of them proceeded on down the bunny hill toward the glorious finish, only to subsequently crash in a tremendous tangle of limbs, rented ski poles, and the sincere desire to simply have the race be over.

As they were sitting there trying to figure out whose arms, legs, and poles belonged to who, they heard a voice scream, "Get the hell out of the way!" which sent both Landgraf and St. Germain scrambling.

The voice belonged to Karl Andresen, who had been Landgraf's political science teacher in college at Eau Claire. Later, Landgraf would move back to Eau Claire and it would be Karl Andresen who would take him under his wing and teach him how to ski, to train, and to eventually love and appreciate the sport.

But on the day of the first Birkie, it was all about survival.

Stumbling to their feet, Landgraf and St. Germain skied up the last little hill to the finish, where an unassuming table sat out in the cold. Landgraf couldn't remember if they were given a medallion or some other trinket, and he was probably too exhausted to care.

Prying off their skis, Landgraf and St. Germain stumbled to the Ratskellar bar at the Telemark lodge and proceeded to order pitcher after pitcher of beer.

"It was the most miserable athletic event that I'd ever been involved in, and I made a vow right then that I would never be talked into any other kind of ridiculous escapade by Ernie," Landgraf said.

He has diligently broken that vow once a year for nearly forty years and counting.

The magic of the Birkie is that is has a way of drawing you back each year for more.

As I was packing up my things and heading out the door, Landgraf nodded with one final thought.

"That phone call from Ernie in 1973 literally changed my life."

Birkie Fever can do that.

The rest of this book tells how it changed mine.

CHAPTER 1

I was seven or eight when I first got on a pair of cross-country skis. When you grow up in Wisconsin, sooner or later you're going to see some skis. You're also going to see Siberian huskies with one blue eye and one brown eye, dead and bloody deer strapped to the hoods of cars, children with bright rosy cheeks fresh in from the cold, and a few Green Bay Packer games. All of these things are equally good in their own particular way, but skis are in a category all their own.

We were living in a little rock house in a town near Madison. It was called Belleville or something like that. I remember the house because it was brown and rocky and miserable and because I once fell down the stairs. I remember thinking it would be awful to die in such an ugly house.

It was Belleville, though, that also provided my first skiing memory. The stone house we lived in was one of those little bumps in the vast wasteland of Midwest nothingness. We were surrounded by fields that were in a constant state of being tilled in the spring and sprouting corn in the summer.

In the fall, we used them for flying kites, dodging the dead stalks that slouched like weary soldiers as we chased the string that inevitably got away from us. Actually, I think I always used to let that string slip out of my hand on purpose because I knew it would get my dad huffing and puffing after it, sprinting through the night like a deranged gorilla that had just escaped from the zoo. It's amazing how much effort a guy will put into getting back a fifty-cent kite. I appreciated him for that.

In the winter, the fields were desert graveyards with miles of windblown snow peaks. Over time they turned into hardened glaciers and I vividly remember the individual snowflakes skittering over them like Styrofoam. The only things that broke the landscape were the skeletal remains of the cornstalks that breached the surface and waved to you like something Melville might imagine, along with the broken barbed-wire fences that stuck out here and there leaving taut, hard lines running straight down beneath the dunes.

It was hell, essentially.

Like some scary uncelebrated level of the underworld.

But, hey! It was home.

One day, my mom whipped out her pair of blue Fischer skis that must have weighed fifty tons each and she put on her wool socks that came up to her knees, followed by her three-pin binder shoes with the big duck bill on the end. All of this action piqued my childish curiosity.

"Hey, Mom, where are you going?"

My mom sighed in annoyance because she'd been going

about these preparations on the sly, probably to get away from me. But I wasn't shrewd enough at that age to be tactful, nor would I have cared to be even if I had been.

"I'm going skiing!"

"Skiing," I asked, "what's that?"

"It's what I'm going to do … ALONE!"

Ha ha! That's what she thought, foolish woman, hadn't she yet learned who ran the house?

I knew where the socks were and I'd learned the trick at least of getting myself quietly prepared without putting up a fuss and guilting her into letting me come along to do this skiing thing, whatever that was.

So upon cutely getting on my socks and looking for a pair of ski boots in the big box of boots and whatnot that had been handed down for seven generations, I, disheveled and adorable as only a seven-year-old can be, looked up at her with my innocent—those are long gone—saucer-like eyes and said with a quivering lip … "P-p-p-lease may I go skiing, too?"

She didn't have a chance.

Lo and behold there were even a pair of pint-sized, shiny red skis in the garage next to her larger ones that looked like a couple of blue whales by comparison. Beside these rested a pair of varnished bamboo poles that were an odd sight in the snow, suggesting, as they did, the warmer climates of their tropical native home.

I pulled on my mittens and examined my poles thoughtfully and remembered a show I'd seen earlier on Disney about some guy who'd built his whole house out of bamboo and I started fantasizing about someday living in a place like that, when my mom broke my concentration.

"Well, are you coming or what?"

She was already outside breaking trail from the garage and it wasn't hard for me to figure out that all I had to do was put my snazzy white-and-red skis into the tracks that she left behind. The miraculous thing was that even though my skis were a third the length of hers, their width fit her tracks just perfectly. So there I was, shuffling along in the bitter cold, getting rosy cheeks and shouting, "Mom … Mom … wait! Wait for me!" To the point where it must have gotten extremely annoying, but, as I mentioned earlier, I didn't understand the concept of "annoying" when I was seven.

So we skied along for awhile in the pastures and the cornfields and the wind blew us and the bits of snow that had somehow gotten picked up upon the breeze cut our cheeks like they always did and in the distance my mom got farther and farther away and I just continued on in my tracks, huffing and puffing like some little abandoned engine, when, all of a sudden, my mom started to get bigger and bigger until I realized she had turned around and was now standing right in front of me.

"What's up?"

"Come on, we're going back."

"Going back?" I said, surprised. I glanced around at my surroundings. I did this not because I was actually looking for anything, but because I had seen adults do it as they reflected on things. It always annoyed me when adults did this because it seemed as if they were only performing the act to waste my time. In vengeance, I was wasting my mom's time. In a surprise twist, however, the contemplation actually produced a thought, and after a just-longer-than-reasonable delay, I stumbled across an idea. "Actually," I said, "I am ready for some hot chocolate."

There was a moment of silence as my mom digested this. It was that moment when you could tell she suspected I was about to become unreasonable, but she wasn't quite sure yet so she wasn't quite angry, but if experience was any indication, she knew she was about to be.

"You can have some hot chocolate when we get back to the house."

I glanced around again in mock reflection. The tension began to rise.

"No," I said flatly, "I want my hot chocolate now. Skiing is fun, but I'm tired of skiing."

My mom's voice went thin as she responded. I had her full attention now and, as any kid will tell you, that's an intoxicating thing. "Well, you have to get back."

"Carry me," I said simply.

The two-word request echoed across the snow-swept field and was met with a reception even frostier than the sub-freezing temperature.

It was the potential utterance of those very words that had provoked my mom to try to sneak out of the house without my knowledge in the first place.

"I'm not going to carry you, you have to ski back."

The response was hard-lipped and absolute, but I wasn't about to back down. At seven, being unreasonable was my prerogative.

I swiveled my bundled body, with the six layers of clothing that were all too big for me, and as I looked into the distance, I could hardly make out our ugly stone house. It must have been a kilometer and a half away.

"I can't make it," I said. "You have to carry me!"

First blood had been drawn in what I assumed was about to be a delightful one- to two-hour argument. I was just settling in to enjoy it when the old bird gave me one heck of a surprise. She didn't even answer me, she just shuffled on by, hopping out of the track—I'd foolishly believed I could block her progress by occupying the trail she had made—and continuing on her way.

"What?!?" I said collapsing to the ground in exhaustion like Madame Bovary.

"I can't make it, it's too far … CARRY ME!"

She just retreated into the distance, leaving me alone to freeze to death with the cornstalks. The wind was already starting to pick up, my little nose went red as the heat began to leave my body.

As the coldness crept into my fingers, I couldn't help but reflect on my life. It had been a good life for the most part, except for that part about falling down the stairs. I hadn't liked that. I also had a complaint about the time I had knelt down next to the exhaust pipe of a car, took an extended whiff and nearly passed out. There was also the time my dad had decided to teach me to play football. His brother had come over and they were in the backyard throwing the leather ball back and forth and I, innocent and excitable, came running out and said, "To me, to me!" and my dad had thrown the ball high in the air, apparently thinking it would be safer that way, and I remember watching it descend, descend, descend, like some wingless bird growing bigger and bigger until it crashed into my face and knocked me flat on my behind with a bloody nose to show for it.

Nope, I didn't catch my first pass.

So I had those three or four solid regrets as I lay there, abandoned by the womb that had carried me, awaiting my death, holding out for my turn to take up my place along the long line of dead cornstalk soldiers … .

"Would you get up and get moving!" my mom screamed from the distance.

Gosh, couldn't a kid even die in peace?

So I struggled to my feet—it was easy back then. Going vertical isn't that difficult when you're four feet tall. And I shuffled forward, sniffling back my tears and heartbreak as I made my way down the weary path. The return journey took longer than the outbound one, and at one point I became fearful that, during the confusion, I might have pointed myself in the wrong direction on the trail. But all it took was a quick glance upward to realize I was nearly home.

The sight of the house excited me and I finished the journey in a rush. I ran inside, bubbling with excitement over my achievement.

"Mom, Mom, did you see that, I must have skied five miles!"

"Yup … "

"That was amazing, did you see me cut through the drifts?"

"Yup … "

"How's my hot chocolate coming along?"

"Right here."

She gave me a mug with two of those tiny little marshmallows that nobody ever uses except in hot chocolate.

It had been a good day.

Any day you get to ski is a good day.

CHAPTER 2

Traumatized from my first bout with skiing, I didn't ski again for five or six years. Oh sure, maybe once or twice when I got a little older and a little better at dressing myself without supervision, I would get mischievous and dig up the old bamboo ski gear and head out for a mini-expedition around the backyard, but it wasn't ever anything memorable.

My next big skiing adventure came when I was twelve or thirteen. There was something new in the air and it was called skate-skiing.

Everybody knows the old-style cross-country skiing, which is now called classical skiing. Classical skiing is the traditional method in which you diagonally stride along with your legs parallel to one another. It's for the purists and for many years it was the only cross-country skiing option. But at one very vivid point in time, the whole cross-country skiing world was turned on its head as a new form of skiing was invented practically out of thin air.

Skate-skiing.

It's exactly what it sounds like—you propel yourself forward by using a roller-blade type skating motion with your legs. It came to be officially known as freestyle skiing, but I think calling it skate-skiing is simpler.

My mom, who had already done a Birkie or so at this point, was showing off her new red-and-white Fischer skis that she had just bought. They were the absolutely first pair of skis that had been designed for skate-skiing and I thought their red-and-white decal job was magnificent. Lighter and more agile than the typical clunky pair of classical skis, these skis also had an aluminum edge that ran down the side like a razor blade for some purpose that only a ski salesman from the mid-eighties could adequately explain.

To make matters better, the old, ugly three-pin bindings were gone. Instead of ugly, duck-billed shoes, my mom had just bought a new pair of slick, sexy ski boots that resembled running shoes.

"Wow!"

"Yeah, wow," Mom said.

"Those look fast!"

"Yeah, fast."

She must have known what was coming next because, at that brief intersection in our history, we had the same size feet.

"Can I try them?"

Once again, silence.

My dad had bought a pair, too, even though he'd only done one Birkie and never let anyone forget how miserable it had been. But still, every time there was some sort of miraculous technological advance, he'd go out and buy the new best thing just to have it, I suppose. I probably could have skied on his equipment—after he bought it, it just rotted in the closet—but his shoes didn't fit and I liked Mom's white ones better than his big red ones anyway.

"No," Mom replied. By then, she had learned how to make a "no" stick.

"Come on!"

"You come on! I just bought these, I want to try them first, at least until I have the new worn off."

Even I had to concede that was valid, which meant I was going to have to reassess my strategy.

"Well, can I ski on your old skis?" I asked.

That got her. I had always been on her case to ski on her old red Fischers, which were also pretty cool. They were still classical skis, but they had a better boot than the old style, three-pin binders.

She paused.

It was all the gap I needed.

"Come on, let me try them and I won't touch your new skis!"

Score.

"But they're classical skis."

"It doesn't matter, I want to try this skating business."

"You can't skate on classical skis."

"Sure you can!"

"You can't! It's not physically possible!"

"Well, somebody must have done it once, or else how did skate-skiing get invented?"

It was a good point, she had to change arguments—which meant I'd won momentum, and would soon win the whole debate.

"You'll ruin the ski!"

"That's absurd."

"No it's not absurd, the camber is for classical and if you start torquing them out, you'll crush all the inner structure."

I didn't know what the hell she was talking about, so I decided to skirt the issue.

"Fine, I'll just classical ski on them."

"You will?"

"Yes."

Lacking further reasonable objection, she had to concede.

I sprinted outside with a quick, "Thanks, Mom," before she could change her mind. Out in the cold, I did a couple quick strides to get the kick wax off and broke out into the skate style like I'd seen on TV. I made it about two strokes before I collapsed like an inverted snow angel into the powder and came up spitting and blowing snow every which way. Undeterred, I tried it two or three more times and must have managed to skate-ski two hundred yards in about forty-five minutes before I crawled, exhausted, back into the house.

"Hey, Mom!"

"Yeah?"

"Just so you know, you can skate-ski on classical skis just fine!"

One of the lovely things of the world is that mothers love their children too much to swat them when they ask for it like that.

CHAPTER 3

By the time we had the skating-on-classical-skis incident, we had already moved from Belleville, on the fringes of Madison, up to Twin Pines, on the fringes of nowhere. Seriously, for those of you in the world who think that Madison, Wisconsin, is as far into the wilderness as you can go, let me let you in on a little secret … Madison is only base camp.

Twin Pines is a town of about 2,000 people way up north of Highway 8 which, like many small towns in frigid climates, proudly boasts approximately two bars per resident. It's mainly known as one of the portals to the Northwoods—a destination people seek out to hunt, fish, and otherwise escape the hustle and bustle of city life. Essentially, Twin Pines is a quiet little community without much cause to garner international attention. However, Twin Pines, does have fame throughout the world as being one of the pit stops on the way to Hayward, a town even smaller and more frontier-like than Twin Pines, but which is, strangely enough, internationally famous for hosting the largest cross-country ski race in the Western hemisphere.

It might seem strange that a town that's even smaller than Twin Pines could manage to put on such an event … but hey, sometimes you start something and it snowballs. That was the case with the American Birkebeiner.

The race was started by Tony Wise to commemorate the Norwegian Birkebeiner, a fifty-four-kilometer event that sends competitors from Rena to Lillehammer.

The Norwegian Birkebeiner itself commemorates a dramatic rescue that occurred during the Civil War era of Norway which took place around the end of the 12th century. The two main parties involved in this war were the Baglers and the Birkebeiners. The Birkebeiners got their name because they used birch bark as gaiters when they went cross-country skiing.

Around 1206, the Baglers targeted the infant Prince Haakon Haakonsson as a threat to their aspirations for the throne of Norway. Aware of the plot and fearful for young Haakon's life, two brave Birkebeiner warriors embarked on a dangerous flight through the rugged wilderness to deliver the young infant to safety. Eventually, Haakon Haakonsson grew up to become king of Norway and put an end to the civil war. Today, in his memory, thousands of people come to Norway every year to do the race while carrying a 3.5-kilogram non-food item to symbolize the baby king in his perilous escape.

I love how they have to specify that it has to be a non-food item. There was surely a day when some joker thought he was beating the system by electing to carry a chocolate baby, only to be disqualified when he arrived at the finish line without the head.

Tony Wise's American Birkebeiner is the same concept as the Norwegian Birkebeiner except you don't have to carry a pseudo-baby. The American version is highly respectful of the historical significance of the race and even elects three people to dress up as Birkebeiner warriors to represent Prince Haakon's mother Inga and the two warriors Torstein and Skervald who carried him. On race day, they do the event like all the rest, but they dress up in furs and ancient weaponry and are required to use wooden skis.

After a decade or so of Wise's tireless promotion, the Birkie bloomed and, as a result, once a year for about a week, the otherwise bland and snow-swept terrain of Northern Wisconsin, with all its lumberjacks, truckers, and bars named after obscure types of swamp brush, becomes infiltrated by cross-country skiers from Norway, Germany, Austria, Australia and pretty much every other country you can think of.

Now, even though I'd grown up in Wisconsin, I still knew of the existence of these exotic-sounding foreign lands. We had a TV after all, and we had a globe with a thousand little countries marked in their appropriate and presumably naturally occurring colors. But it is a much different thing to see people pretending to be from a different country on the television than it is to actually sit down to breakfast with a real-life foreign traveler in a small cafe just a few blocks from your home.

I learned pretty quickly that the TV got just about everything wrong.

People from foreign countries talk differently for one

thing, especially when they break off from the polite conversation they're having with the locals and say a couple words to one another in what sounds like a bunch of meaningless clicks and whistles. You would swear these sounds didn't mean anything at all until, suddenly, the whole group would simultaneously break out into laughter, causing you to presume you were somehow the punchline.

But apart from that, these fascinating travelers perceived things that I never would have thought to notice. They asked weird questions like, "Why is every entree in this country served with an identical quarter-slice of miserable-looking pickle?" Questions like these had an oddly resounding logic even though it had never occurred to me to ask the same thing. These otherwordly visitors delighted in the fact that they could pay for their meals by leaving their money on the table and walking out the door. After a little while all these little quirks and differences combined and multiplied in my mind to bring forth a whole new realm of possibilities to consider.

Why was leaving money on the table so unique?

Don't they do it that way everywhere?

Don't they eat pickles in Australia?

Oh my gosh … what else is different in the places where these people come from?

I suppose you can see how once you start thinking like this and apply it over a couple of days or weeks, the person who comes out at the end has far different ambitions and motivations than the one who had until recently been accepting everything at face value.

Every year these international travelers would come for a week and the Northwoods would be alive and chirping with a thousand voices speaking in such a strange and magnificent variety of sounds that I became overwhelmed with a profound sense of how ridiculously grand and diverse the world really is.

And then they'd be gone.

Absent long enough that I began thinking that their appearance must have been a dream. That it couldn't have been real. That I'd imagined it all.

And just when I'd convinced myself that I'd made it all up, they all came back, chirping and talking incomprehensibly and laughing away.

And skiing.

All for skiing.

If that was what the Birkie was all about, I knew I was going to have to ski it someday.

CHAPTER 4

The Birkie is a fundamental part of Hayward and my grandfather was a fairly respected member of the Hayward community. He'd been a doctor in the area for years, long enough that he could surprise young ladies who were working at restaurants by sauntering up to them and saying, "I've seen you naked." He usually let the strange comment linger in the air for a few awkward seconds as the girls tried to figure out whether he was a pervert or crazy, and then he'd cackle, "I delivered you!" Then he'd laugh for about fifteen minutes in a way that he thought dissolved the goofy creepiness of the moment but really only abated about seven percent of it.

Grandpa was an acquired taste.

I personally thought he was funny as hell.

His house sat on the shores of Hayward Lake. During Birkie season, you could watch the skiers coming in all day long. Grandpa and Grandma used to sit next to the bay window in the kitchen and cheer them in.

Sometimes during the random, boring nights on Hayward Lake, Grandpa would dig around in his closet until he found the tracer rounds that he'd brought back from World War II. He would shoot them across the water, giggling wildly the whole time. It was the type of thing only the elderly are allowed to get away with because everybody is afraid to arrest them.

Back in those days, the Birkie office had a program in which elite skiers could stay with Hayward families and get a little local color while saving on lodging. Grandpa signed up to take a couple Birkie skiers, and the Birkie office, knowing what a respected person my Grandpa was, rewarded him with two decorated skiing champions, Manfred Nagl and Rudy Kapeller.

Rudy Kapeller had won the Birkie in 1983 and when you were around him, you could feel the presence of the thousands of frigid kilometers the guy had charged mercurially through. Although he'd come out the other end safe and sound, he had nonetheless been changed by the experience. Hard-core skiers have a hardness about them. Their eyes are narrowly focused as if they're in a constant state of picking out the best line to take to get down a steep hill a half-mile away. If you're right next to them, they don't really notice you because they're about to go sprinting off toward the horizon. But if you're a half-click in the distance, you're the entire focus of their attention, and until they've picked you off, they see nothing else.

Rudy was Austrian, and he remains to this day a well known and respected ambassador to the country and to the sport.

On this trip to the Birkie, he wasn't favored to win. The

odds were on his prodigy, Manfred Nagl. Manfred was an Austrian police officer. He was a huge guy, and can still be seen in the occasional ski lodge in the area, charging to the finish with his mustache leading the way on a Birkie Poster from '90 or '91.

There are two things I vividly remember from Manfred's and Rudy's visit to my Grandpa's house.

The first is the morning of the Birkie when the two of them were testing their glide on a small hill outside the living room window. Although testing glide is obvious for anybody who has skied a race, having not yet attempted it, I found it interesting to watch these two world-class athletes ride their skis about fifty feet, whip them off, try another pair, judge the distance and the feel, and stand there and discuss the results heatedly like a pair of German-speaking chipmunks.

The other thing I remember was how my Grandpa took them out in his massive Buick to teach them how not to drive on ice. Somehow I got dragged along on that ill advised adventure as well.

He loaded us into his car and was quiet except for an internal, full-body chuckle that indicated he was tickled by something he was planning to do. He said little until we left the driveway and merged onto the road, which was filled with obstacles like oncoming traffic and pedestrians.

"This is ice," he said as the four of us drove along. "It's black ice."

"Ja," said Manfred, probably not really understanding.

"Ja," said Rudy, also probably not really understanding.

"Black ice is really dangerous because you can't see it," Grandpa continued, speaking like Willy Wonka, his eyes twinkling mischievously.

"Ja."

"Ja."

I just sat there with my seatbelt fastened. I had learned a long time ago that you just had to go along with Grandpa, because if you tried to stop him, things really got out of hand.

"The absolute last thing you ever want to do on black ice is THIS!"

Cackling wildly, Grandpa jammed his leg onto the brakes as hard as he could. The car skidded toward a ditch, fishtailing out of control.

Manfred and Rudy's highly conditioned reflexes took over, and both their arms snapped to the seats in front of them as their eyes widened in terror. Other than that, they did nothing. No screaming, no protesting, nothing. Their reaction was really quite impressive—it made me wonder what those Austrians had been through in their lives to be able to react so calmly to this.

"And you never want to do this!" Grandpa continued as he spun the wheel furiously this way and that, slamming alternately on the gas and the brakes, causing the vehicle to lurch at the ditch, back onto the road, back toward the other ditch, and finally spin a full 360 degrees out of control. All the while, Grandpa laughed hysterically.

After about two eternities, the car jerked to a halt.

Manfred and Rudy gave each other a slow, almost imperceptible glance.

Neither one of them said "Ja" again, but Grandpa didn't notice. He just drove us back to the house, chuckling all the way.

"I taught them how *not* to drive on black ice," he said to Grandma as he entered.

"Oh, dear," Grandma replied. From the way she'd said it, I was sure that she had also been "taught" how not to drive on black ice on more than one terrifying occasion.

Manfred Nagl went on to win the Birkie that year.

From what I remember, he went straight through the finish line and skied all the way to the Minneapolis airport without even stopping to change his clothes. It must not have been that traumatic, however, because he did come back to win the Birkie two more times, though he didn't stay at Grandpa's house again.

CHAPTER 5

I had already been inspired by the presence of the Birkie, but the Manfred Nagl episode really got me going. As usual, I took it out on my poor mom.

"Mom, I need some skis!"

"Use the little red ones!"

"The little red ones are two feet long! I need some man-sized skis." I was all of fifteen at the time.

"Grrrrrrr … ."

Actually, my mom was always keen to go to the ski shop and peruse the items, but she was too much of a wily veteran to let on that my request was something she actually wanted to do. It's always better to lay low and resist in any negotiation, only capitulating after wrestling out some sort of ridiculous concession for your generosity. This is in line with how I've never admitted to my wife that I like *Rambo* as much as she does. We watch it every time it comes on, but only on the condition that it counts as one of *her* movies.

About a half-hour later, we were on our way to the ski shop. I was pumped about the fact that I'd be getting some new cross-country skis.

"I'm going to get a pair of Fischers just like yours."

Mom nearly choked on her coffee.

"My Fischers are the best pair of skis made."

"Exactly!"

"You've skied, what … three times in your life? What makes you think you deserve the best skis?"

"I'm a natural."

"They're expensive!"

"Only the best for your kids!"

She sank in her seat, realizing she would never get the best deal when bargaining with her own child.

At the ski shop, I went straight to the rack of Fischers. They were long and sleek like Arabian horses, or finely tuned, muscular athletes. I lifted them, only to discover that they had no weight. It was amazing. I looked down and was startled to realize they were chained to the floor—obviously! Imagine the expense the store would incur if they just let their product float up to heaven where it belonged.

"They're beautiful," I said, a tear coming to my eye.

"They're four hundred and fifty dollars," grunted my mom.

How sad it was to have her blatant materialism ruin such a perfect moment.

"But these are the skis I must have."

"Alright."

"Alright?"

I was suspicious. It was never that easy. I looked at her. She shrugged.

"Well, I figure I can loan you the money."

"Loan?"

"Yeah, loan. And you can work it off doing chores around the house. I figure you'll have these paid off in a year or two."

My eyes narrowed. So she had been thinking as she sat quietly behind the steering wheel.

Our haggling was interrupted by a cough.

"Maybe I can help?" It was the salesman. He was one of those young, lean, skier-looking guys that are always hanging out in ski shops.

"Yeah," I said. "What's on sale?"

In the end, I had realized nothing was more beautiful than freedom.

He trotted us over to a rack of pale blue Rossignols. I gave them an appraising and disappointed look, but secretly I didn't think they were too bad. On the tips was an animal that looked like a chicken. I presumed that was the Rossi logo. The Fischers had three equilateral triangles stacked to make one larger, bigger triangle. It looked like the warning symbol for nuclear power as if your skis were trying to say, "Watch out, if you stand too close to this guy, you might go sterile."

Rossis had a chicken …

But the thing was, it was kind of a cool chicken. It had a blue, white and red vertical stripe and the whole thing was framed by a glittering gold outline. Sure, it didn't have the brute force of the Fischer logo, but it was strangely and comically elegant.

Meanwhile the salesman was doing his thing by picking up the skis—these weren't chained down—and talking about their miraculous, high-tech features.

"These solid red bases are the latest in wax-absorbing polymer, and these two offset vertical grooves have taken the place of the traditional single groove because the scientists at Rossignol have determined that this construction will provide greater handling and stability."

"Two grooves?"

"Yes."

"And this is the way the industry is going?"

"Absolutely, in two or three years, every skate-ski will have two grooves instead of just one."

"My mom's Fischers have an aluminum edge running down the sides."

The salesman laughed.

"An absurd idea, it will never appear on a pair of skis again."

My mom looked down dejectedly.

"They work great in icy conditions," she said defiantly.

The salesman was smart enough not to say anything.

"How much?"

"Package deal of skis, poles, bindings and boots for $250."

Oh well, they weren't Fischers, but the price was right. I'd only be working for about six months.

"Sold."

On the way home I had to tease my mom about the fact that I'd be skiing on superior technology with my two vertical grooves.

"Well, I have aluminum edges."

"They never worked the way they were supposed to," I said dismissively.

"Who says?"

"The salesman said!"

"Ah, what does he know!"

Secretly I agreed with her and still thought her aluminum-edged Fischers were the coolest skis in the world. But I was on Rossis now, and I had to defend my hardware—skiers get strangely attached to their brands, and they defend them with an unreasonable obsession.

CHAPTER 6

As excited as I was about my new Rossis, sadly, I was not to write a great story upon them. Cross-country skiing is a treacherous mistress, and she's apt to throw you a couple of loops before you figure her out. Indeed, most outsiders looking in think cross-country folks are completely crazy.

"What's fun about skiing uphill?"

"You go out when it's negative twenty-five degrees, wearing nothing but a Lycra suit?"

"What the hell is a kilometer anyway?"

These are the types of things screamed out by snowmobilers as they roar by in a cloud of gasoline and beer fumes, sometimes ruining our preciously groomed and prepared trails in the process.

Finding the "fun" in cross-country can be difficult.

It's cold.

It's physically daunting.

Doing it is nearly impossible. Most experts claim it takes about five years to really develop good skiing technique. Perfecting your technique takes a lifetime.

This is why I tell people that if they're thinking of taking up cross-country, they should do it in late February or March.

Late February when the sun has somewhat returned to the sky after the long, cold winter.

March when the temperatures always hover somewhere close to freezing or blessedly above.

Go skiing on a flat course and increase your chances of finding the fun.

Do not, however, pick the shortest day of the year. A dark, terrifying demon of a day in late December, when the sun is already sprinting to the west at 2:30 in the afternoon. A day when the mercury only reaches negative twenty-something degrees before giving up and falling back to the wide receptacle at the bottom of the glass. Don't go out when the wind is ninety-five miles per hour from the north, carrying baseball-sized chunks of ice that beat you to a pulp like that famous dairy machine that blows the holes through the Swiss cheese. And whatever you do, on your first ski, don't go up to the Birkie trail and go north of OO, where the hills buckle like a serpent's tail and the snapping maw seems to lurk in the distance, waiting for you to show the slightest tremor of weakness so it can whip around, snatch you up and swallow you whole.

And don't take your kids out on days like this, either.

Or they'll crawl into the car, beaten and destroyed after

having come to look at their skis—no matter how new and shiny they are—as clamped-on instruments of torture. They'll peel them off, throw them in the back and sit down and watch TV for a week or a year, or maybe forever.

Everybody has a hard training day from time to time, it's just something you have to put into perspective.

Finding the fun with skiing is a bit of a challenge. The fun side is an elusive beast, you have to sneak up on it using guile and stealth. It's a glorious sight to behold, but until you do, cross-country can seem like a pitiless, leering monster waiting in the wilderness like a Nordic troll.

When you finally do see it, it's as timid as a bunny rabbit.

The greatest of joys.

And you become hot with the fever of it.

But like I said, finding the fun the first time can be quite a trick.

CHAPTER 7

For a few years, Birkie fever dwindled in me and I pursued other interests. It took a backhoe, of all things, to rekindle my desire. I was plodding my way through Twin Pines High School, which didn't offer the diversity of opinion necessary for a young soul who had already had a small taste of distant and exotic places.

In art class at Twin Pines, a still life meant you were painting a picture of a duck.

Or a whitetail.

Or a musky.

There simply were no other art subjects.

If you asked the teacher about Van Gogh, or Salvador Dali, or Jackson Pollock, he just sighed, defeated.

"Not too much use for those names around here."

It wasn't his fault, it was just the system.

Life was strange in Twin Pines, everything seemed upside-down.

So when I graduated, I lacked direction, although probably not any more than the typical 18-year-old recent graduate. I enrolled in college for a while, but it didn't sit well with me, so I quit the first week, much to the displeasure of everyone, as you might imagine. Contrary to popular thought, it is possible to return to college after taking a year off. The hard part is putting up with everyone's sideways looks for that year.

I started working at the cranberry marsh in Seeley, Wisconsin, just north of Hayward. There are a million cranberry marshes in the Twin Pines/Hayward area. I was living at home and spending no more money than it cost me to drive to and from work. Although it was miserable at the time, working for a year and spending zero dollars set me up pretty well for the near future.

Marsh work was pretty generic; it was a good place to be left alone. On one occasion, it was my job to dig a big ditch with a million-dollar backhoe. If you've never spent a ten-hour day in a backhoe, you haven't missed anything. I even listened to Rush Limbaugh for company for about five seconds until I realized silence was more profound. Slowly, alone in the backhoe, you go mad. Take my word for it.

So I was digging this big ditch. I don't know what for. They said, "Dig a big ditch."

I said, "Where?"

They said, "Over there."

I said, "With what?"

They said, "This million-dollar backhoe. Be careful with it."

I said, "OK."

So I started digging away, kind of falling asleep all the while. When you're operating a backhoe, you just work the controls and after a little bit of time has passed it starts to feel like a video game. The day goes by in a pleasant, surreal blur until you accidentally jerk the handle too quickly and dislodge a big rock that comes crashing into the window you've been staring out of. Sitting there, covered in shards of broken glass, you get a harsh reminder that this isn't a video game, this is real life.

The bad thing about reality, as compared to video games, is that you only get one chance to get it right. There aren't additional lives to pick up after achieving fantastic point totals. In real life, it's one and done. It's kind of terrifying if you stop and think about it, so I recommend not thinking about it whenever possible.

So after we got the window fixed, the boss came up to me and said, "Remember what I said about being careful with the million-dollar backhoe?"

I said, "Yeah."

He said, "That still goes."

There I was again, digging the ditch and it was getting nice and deep. You could sit there and dig all day, all you saw was rocks and dirt. The only fun parts were those moments of terror when the rocks came flying at you, but I had been encouraged to avoid those. You could also swing the backhoe back and forth really fast and smash the back end of the machine into the big mound of dirt you were piling up. That was kind of fun, but I found out later that doing this put a big dent in the body of the machine and filled the engine with a fine sand that clogged up the works. That isn't recommended treatment for a million-dollar backhoe.

So one day, I was almost entirely in a daze when I did something I didn't realize was possible. I was still digging this big hole and I was on the edge of it. The hole was as deep as the backhoe was tall, and as wide as twice the length of the backhoe. It was a darn big hole. I was starting to be proud of it. Maybe millions of years later, people would come and look at my hole and say, "Man, that's a nice hole. That's the only hole you can see from outer space, you know."

I was in my typical daze, half-asleep, half-awake, working the controls and taking big scoops of dirt from below. I wanted the walls of my hole to be perfectly vertical. I thought that was the mark of a well crafted excavation. It didn't deter me that I was digging in sand, which doesn't hold its form as well as black dirt—I was going to make my wall rise ninety degrees from the ground. So I scraped my bucket along the bottom and brought it up the wall that was just outside my window. Almost instantly, the sand rolled off the wall and back into the bottom of the ditch. Not really thinking, I just kept going after it with my backhoe bucket. I did this again and again, until I swung the bucket around and imagined that I felt the backhoe teeter.

Icy fear ran through my body. *What's happening?* I

thought frantically. I sat still, doing nothing for a few seconds. I had learned quickly while running a backhoe that when things start to go wrong, it is a good idea to let go of the controls. If you start jerking on them wildly, you are apt to kill people.

A few minutes passed. Rush Limbaugh said something inane. I decided all was well. I turned the backhoe around again and took another big scoop from right underneath myself, not recognizing the inherent stupidity of this maneuver. I began to turn the bucket to dump the load when the backhoe started not just to teeter, but to actually topple over into the hole! I broke my magic rule about not touching the controls in an emergency and slammed the bucket down into the excavation to prop up the machine from falling. Images of the million-dollar backhoe tumbling head over heels into the pit filled my mind. A million-dollar crumpled piece of junk.

Slamming the bucket into the hole stopped the plunge. I sat there, panting. After a few moments, everything seemed stable and I jumped out of the machine to have a look. Most backhoes move on two parallel treads, like a bulldozer. The cabin with the digging arm swivels on top. My treads were situated parallel to the hole. It would have been fine except that most of the dirt under one of the treads had crumbled away into the ditch. The backhoe looked ridiculous, propped up by its arm and resting on only one tread with earth beneath it.

"Dang," I said. At this point, it probably would have been prudent to call somebody who was competent and ask for help. But I didn't feel like admitting my mistake. I didn't want to get stuck doing a job that involved walking around or anything. So I valiantly decided to take my life in my hands and climbed back into the machine. Slowly, I pushed on the two levers that operated the treads. The backhoe shuddered and moved. The arm was still slammed into the ground for support. After I had moved a little way, I let go of the levers and slid the arm across the bottom of the hole. This kept the supporting arm under the center of mass. I was terrified the whole time. I thought at any moment, the rest of the wall would give way and my backhoe would go tumbling to its and my ultimate destruction. I moved the levers again, then I moved the bucket. Bit by bit, like an old man walking with a cane, I got that machine onto stable ground. I lifted the bucket and fled the scene at five miles per hour, as fast as a backhoe can go. Then I parked the backhoe a short distance away and rested in a cold sweat.

I wondered if Manfred Nagl had ever been in a similar situation.

At that point, I decided two things.

One was that I was going to go back to college since I didn't want to end up digging holes all my life.

The other was that I was going to ski the Birkie, because at least that was something significant and I was feeling short on significance at that moment. These are the resolutions you are forced to make when you essentially fail as a ditch digger.

CHAPTER 8

My first Birkie was a big event, and the prospect terrified me. It terrified me so much, in fact, that I didn't sign up right away. I wanted to wait and see if I could get into any kind of skiing shape. What I didn't know was that the price of the Birkie went up by like 300 percent each day leading up to the race. Word to the wise—pre-register. This is even more relevant now, since these days registration closes several months before the day of the race.

My old blue Rossis didn't fit me anymore, so I prowled around the house looking for some skis. I was sure that if I failed to find skis in the box of whatnot that had been handed down for generations, then the odds were pretty good I'd find a pair in some hidden closet or something. Most houses are full of stuff people have forgotten about and stored away — you'd be surprised at some of the things you can find in the closets of your own home.

But this time I had a purpose. I knew what I was looking for—my dad's top-of-the-line skis that he had never used. I embarked on my search and three or four dusty alcoves later I emerged victorious, a pair of Fischer skis and Solomon boots only about a year old clutched in my hands. A mouse was living in one of the boots, but I moved him out and was ready to ski.

This was a significant moment for me since it underscored a commitment to the enterprise. I'd always played around with skiing before, but now skiing meant something.

I was in kind of a post-high school funk and not too happy about the way things were going at work or in life. At eighteen, I hadn't yet learned that life is a never ending roller-coaster of highs and lows, and I didn't know to have faith in the inevitable rebound. Instead, I felt as if I was on the edge of the precipice and was about to tumble into a world of monotony and manual labor from which I'd never be able to escape. I had to do something that set me apart, something to allow me to believe that I was different and that I had some value.

I needed something to hang my hat on, something to separate me.

And believe me, nobody at that cranberry marsh had any intentions skiing the Birkie.

The image of the hoary beast from those unfortunate skiing misadventures of my youth still lurked in the back of my mind and gave me pause. The frigid pines of the trail north of OO still made me tremble. I lacked the physical fitness, the proper clothing, the waxing skills and the technique, but my back was against the wall.

I was going to be a skier!

I had to be.

Training was tough while working forty hours a week doing manual labor. The good news was that the cranberry marsh was right next to the Birkie trail, so I could stop off and ski right after work. The bad news was that I was always dirty and exhausted after putting in my 8 hours.

I would pull into "00" in my ripped jeans and wool shirt and hammer out a few kilometers. Back then, it wasn't much to look at. I'd totter back and forth on my skis and everybody —I mean everybody—would pass me.

I don't care how Zen you are, when everybody's passing you at some athletic enterprise, you get a little frustrated and punchy.

I started hating the faster skiers.

I thought of them as rude.

I thought of them as aloof.

I found myself playing mini-games of chicken with them as I refused to give ground either as oncoming traffic or when they tried to pass me.

It was envy, of course, as it was infuriating to watch them dance up the hills, floating over the terrain like mystical beings free from the pull of the Earth.

I, in contrast, was a lumbering beast with motor oil on my jeans and gnarled, scratchy hair on my face.

We occupied the same place out there on the Birkie trail, but our worlds could not have been more different.

I suppose I skied aggressively because I wanted to prove that I belonged. But it was a misplaced aggression because it wasn't them I needed to convince, it was myself.

I struggled to get in my ten kilometers, skiing out five kilometers and coming back in the dark. This was before the days of the lit trails.

Back in my car, I'd turn up the heat and drive home, not bothering to change out of my cold, wet clothes. I'd arrive at my house, go straight to bed, wake up at four a.m. and start the whole process all over again.

It wasn't ideal training, but it was enough to get me to the finish line.

At least I hoped it was enough.

CHAPTER 9

That year, the Birkie office had finally forgiven Grandpa over the Manfred Nagl affair and he had been rewarded with a group of Australians who were coming up to do the event. Fearful for their sanity, my mom made an effort to get them away from Grandpa as often as possible by taking them skiing and around town. I tagged along as well for a couple reasons—one was that I was trying to get in shape for skiing, the other was that one of the Australians was a girl my age named Kathryn.

On one occasion we were all sitting around the table at Coop's Pizza. If you don't know Coop's, you should make an effort to check it out. It's simply the best pizza in the universe. However, when you're in super-serious ski-training mode, you can't afford the luxury of eating pizza. Instead, we were eating Coop's equally delectable chicken breast sandwiches. For an extra dollar, you could get your sandwich with two chicken breasts. The resulting stack made the sandwich too big to get into your mouth, which was exactly how I like my sandwiches.

The oldest of the Australians was a math teacher

named Rob. He basically knew the entire Australian ski community, including the Olympians. This fact amazed me since I'd always thought of Olympic athletes as superior beings who lived on a cloud mountain in the midst of some fantasy realm and only indulged in the mortal world for the purposes of recreational intercourse and to procure Olympic medals. As I've said before, my fantasies are often much better than reality.

But Australia is a small enough country, and those who practice the sport of cross-country skiing are such a limited group that those with Olympic dreams have more of a cozy fraternity than it sometimes feels like here in the states.

Our conversation on that afternoon, however, had nothing to do with the Olympics. Instead, Rob was fascinated by the slice of pickle that accompanied his Coop's sandwich.

"Why is it," he said in his quaint Australian accent, "that every restaurant here in the U.S. serves everybody the identical miserable, dried-up, horrible-looking pickle? Why must every plate I order be garnished with this pathetic, slug-like item? Why? Look at the plates as they go back to the kitchen! Nobody eats the pickle! Why do they serve it?"

As he said it, I realized that it was kind of true. I'd never eaten that pickle and I didn't know anybody who had. Why *did* they keep serving it? Maybe they should have made it an option. They should have a little box you could check that said "with or without pickle."

Suddenly, Rob turned to face my mom. "You know what your dad's been up to?" he said slyly. After staying with my grandparents for a few days, everybody had stories.

Instinctively, my mom covered her face in embarrassment.

"Don't tell me … "

Rob started to smile as his eyes rolled back in his head to recount the moment.

"This morning your dad pulled me into the hallway and presented me with a revolver."

Prepared as she was for anything, Rob's words still took her by surprise.

"No! He gave you a gun?" she gasped. Rob started to chuckle.

"Not as a gift," Rob clarified. "He wanted me to shoot it."

The corners of Rob's mouth began to quiver with suppressed laughter; the sensation was contagious among those gathered at the table. Even Mom began to chuckle as her initial shock ebbed.

"Let me guess," she said with resignation. "He gave you the old line about rubber bullets."

Rob nodded solemnly and a few giggles escaped the falsely stern mask he wore. He then threw his voice into a fairly good imitation of my Grandpa and said, "I've got some targets set up down the hall by the bathroom, go ahead and shoot them. Don't worry, the gun's loaded with rubber bullets!"

"He then shoved the gun into my chest," Rob continued in his own voice.

"Wait," I interrupted, "he wanted you to shoot the gun down the hallway?"

"Yes," Rob replied simply.

"At the targets?"

"Yes."

"With rubber bullets?"

"Yes."

We broke into peals of laughter. For a minute, we couldn't contain our mirth as we imagined our dignified Australian guest standing in my grandpa's house trying to figure out if he would be committing some tremendous affront to Wisconsin sensibilities by refusing to fire a handgun indoors.

The burden of being a good houseguest is a sacred trust. I didn't envy the difficult choice Rob had been presented with.

"Well," my mom asked, "did you?"

Rob threw her a priceless look. It was a mixture of derision and helplessness, self-loathing and delighted mischief. Rob held the moment for a long time, allowing the tension to build.

"Of all the people in this world," he said, his gaze fixed on my mom, "you know how insistent your father can be. Of course I shot the targets, I had to shoot the targets! When your dad wants something to happen, it happens."

We laughed so hard I thought they were going to throw us out of the restaurant. I began to wonder if Grandpa had pulled the same trick on Manfred Nagl and Rudy Kapeller when they had stayed at his house. Presenting your guests with a gun is a difficult enough situation to handle when you know they speak the same language as you. If you're dealing with a language barrier on top of all the other cultural differences, firearms simply aren't going to simplify the situation.

When we finally caught our breaths, I realized there were still questions to be answered.

"Well," I asked, "were there really rubber bullets in the gun or did you blow a hole in the wall?"

"I don't really know," Rob confessed, "a second after the gun went off, everything went black. I don't remember a thing after that."

None of us believed that, but try as we might, we couldn't pry any more information out of Rob. In the end we had to conclude that either he was just being coy or the event really had become truly traumatic.

Every time we saw Rob thereafter, he had a new story of my Grandpa's antics. But unlike Manfred Nagl, Rob kept coming back year after year.

Australians know how to party a little better than Austrians, apparently (or maybe it was just the language thing).

"You know," Rob confided to my mom once, "I stay at your parents' house for a week and I have stories for dinner parties for the next five years."

CHAPTER 10

I was having a good time showing the younger Australians around. They were all good skiers and it was fun to interlope in their world. Along with Kathryn, Ethan and Rob, there were a couple more Australians in the area doing local events. I taught them how to play American football and took Ethan to a local basketball game so he could have a look at some real American cheerleaders.

He wasn't that impressed.

"They don't look like the ones in the movies," he said grumpily.

"They never do," I replied.

I was still going to work and digging ditches or driving a dump truck, but it was fun to come home and hang out with the Australians, who took to staying at our house … all but Rob, that is, who secretly enjoyed my grandparents too much.

There was enough going on that I wasn't obsessing over the Birkie even though it was rapidly approaching.

I still hadn't signed up, although there was little doubt that I was going to do it. I'd been talking about it with everybody, and spending all my time hanging out with skiers. I was becoming part of their community and that was too precious to give up.

But one challenge remained.

The Saturday before the Birkie, I headed up to the trail all by myself. Months earlier, I had determined this would be the ultimate test.

I pulled into OO, the site of so many training days, and sat in the car thoughtfully as I pulled on my, or rather my dad's, ski boots.

South of OO beckoned, but I knew that route all too well. That was the civilized part of the trail. OO itself was the end of the Kortelopet, the half-length Birkie race. From OO on, it was a mellow, almost downhill run to Hayward with only a couple big hills to serve as bumps in the road.

The challenge lay to the north, where the highest point of the trail, the top of the divide, waited amongst the pines. If you can ski north of OO up to Telemark, you're in sufficient shape to do the Birkie.

That was my plan for the day.

I jumped out of the car and hit the trail, again in jeans and a wool shirt. There was nothing fancy about my equipment, except my skis, which were a top-model set of Fischers. But they were about ten centimeters too long, my boots were a size too big and my poles were about five centimeters too short.

But I had enough to ski.

I don't remember much about that journey up the divide. It was a decent day, not too cold or warm, with a little snowfall. Climbing the divide is a beast. But when I started feeling overwhelmed, I just put my mind elsewhere and carried on.

I was in a new place now than I had been even a few months before. There were images in my mind that had replaced the burned-in scene of a backhoe cockpit or the steering wheel of a dump truck. Now I was thinking of Australia, I was thinking of laughing girls with chipper accents, I was thinking of brilliant white snow and people dancing across it in brightly colored uniforms.

And I was a part of it.

I hit the divide and kept right on going. Down the backside of the hill that few people see except on race day. I was in no-man's land of the Birkie trail. The terrain was far too difficult for casual training, so only the really dedicated skiers ever ventured to that region.

The dedicated skiers and me.

I hit the twenty-kilometer-point from OO, exhausted, and I stopped. I took off my skis, sat down in the ice, and watched the sky, which had just begun to light up with the downward path of the sun.

I pulled an orange from my pocket and sat there eating it reflectively. Amazingly, it hadn't frozen along the way. The fruit was as sweet and magical as it can be only after you've just made a grand physical exertion.

I remember that moment clearly, because suddenly it became obvious that I was going to make it. I was hopeful for the first time in a long while.

The moment lingered, and then went, and I stood up to ski the rest of the way back, undeterred that I had sentenced myself to skiing at least some of the distance in the dark.

I don't remember the return journey, but I must have made it since I'm sitting here writing this today.

CHAPTER 11

A couple days before the Birkie, we went and got our bibs at Telemark. This was the moment when you turned in the little card you get in the mail after registering—I'd registered at the Birkie office in Hayward shortly after my forty-kilometer divide ski—and you receive your awesome Birkie bib in return.

Birkie bibs are a big deal.

They look a lot like baby bibs except they're bigger, they cover your front and back, and they're numbered. The bib color indicates your wave. There are so many people who want to do the Birkie that you can't set them all off at once. From a distance, a cross-country skier looks a little bit like a mosquito—beautiful long, delicate limbs, extended by the length of their skis and poles. Individually, they are elegant and fragile, but when you put a thousand of them in a jar and shake it up, you can imagine the chaos that occurs—the resulting mess is similar to a massive pile of tangled coat hangers.

For that reason, the Birkie separates the start into waves of about eight hundred people, and these waves are assigned based on Birkie finish times. First-time Birkie skiers like me were assigned to the last wave. I was assigned to wave eight, which had an ugly brown bib. My mom was in wave three, which was a pretty light blue.

I had dreams of moving up a couple waves, but I kept reminding myself that this was a building year.

Kathryn and her brother were also assigned to wave three due to their status as international skiers. Olympic-level skiers were assigned to the "elite" wave, which was the first two hundred (three hundred in some years) finishers from the previous year, and any other "contender" who wanted to do the race.

Birkie skiers tend to treasure their Birkie bibs. I've been to homes where people dig out their twenty-plus Birkie bibs and hang them on the rafters like Christmas decorations. I've known other families who have sewn their Birkie bibs into quilts.

The faces of most Birkie bibs are white, with a few exceptions. People who have completed twenty Birkies become members of the Birchleggings club and are awarded a purple bib, and skiers who have done thirty or more Birkies get a light gold bib. But the best bibs are the red Founders bibs, awarded to skiers who have skied every single Birkie.

I was pretty psyched about getting my first Birkie bib. It had a big "1" stamped in the corner so the volunteers at the finish line would know that I was to get a medal —subsequent years received pins.

In fact, everybody—by which I mean the Australians and me—was pretty psyched about getting a Birkie bib; so psyched, in fact, that we, two days before the race mind you, decided to play some football. Back when I was younger, spontaneous games of football used to break out around me with startling frequency. This was mostly because I forced anyone I came into contact with to play football sooner or later. Still, football a couple days before an endurance skiing event is not a very good mix.

After about a three-hour game, I limped back into the house with a mildly pulled hamstring, shaking my head at my own stupidity.

It hurt, and I had only two days to recover.

Birkie fever makes you do silly things. However, not racing is never considered an option.

CHAPTER 12

Race day is so fast, you only remember it in hindsight.

Above all, you have to get up early.

Super early.

Ridiculously early.

You've got to get up early because everybody's heading out to the Birkie trail and you don't want to be left behind.

Can't be late.

Don't want to be late.

You get up at approximately four in the morning and you look for your clothing.

What's the temperature?

Are my skis going to be OK?

You look out the window at the thermometer and see that it's four degrees.

Oh no!

You waxed for twenty!

Your skis are going to be slow! You aren't going to make it! It's going to be terrible!

You whip out the iron and you're about to put some different wax on the skis when somebody stops you.

Oh yeah, it's four a.m., it's going to warm up!

On to other things, like breakfast.

Gotta eat! Gotta eat!

I'm too nervous to eat, nothing will stay down.

A bagel?

Get that out of my face!

Cereal?

That won't give you energy for two kilometers!

Oatmeal?

It sticks to the inside of your throat like the tentacles of an octopus … it makes you gag!

Some plain spaghetti noodles?

OK, let's give that a try.

You suck them down.

They don't squirm much … you're good to go.

Something like five or five-thirty, you're out the door, on the way.

It's dark.

A row of cars threads a trail up to Hayward like the last scene from "Field of Dreams."

The car warms up as you drive.

Music plays.

You get to Hayward.

A huge field has been plowed out for you to park in.

Guys are standing in it with glowing wands guiding you to where you can stick your vehicle.

They motion you forward.

Will I remember where my car is?

How am I getting back here?

No time for questions like this.

Out of the car and onto the bus.

The Australians are excited.

Why are they excited?

The bus is like the bus from *The Simpsons*!

Arriving at Telemark.

It's seven-thirty now.

Take off the warm-up jacket.

Use the bathroom again.

Lines are long, there goes another hour.

The race has started by now, the elites are gone, the first wave is gone.

The Australians and Mom are heading out in wave three.

Waiting outside, shivering.

Wave four, wave five, wave six.

It's thin khakis instead of oil-stained jeans. Gotta look stylish for the Birkie.

Wave seven, here we go.

They shoot a firework into the air.

Out of it bursts smoke and an American flag.

"They're burning the flag!" you say indignantly.

A few people laugh.

Starting gun!

BOOM!

And you ski.

Down the power lines.

Into the hills.

The downhills have ruts from people snowplowing.

The masses are huge, you stand in line to climb hills.

People all around.

You ski.

Up the divide.

I recognize this part of the trail!

Down.

Snowmobilers stand at a sharp corner and laugh at everyone.

You continue.

On to OO.

More than half the skiers evaporate at the Korteloppet finish.

Ahhh, you finally have some elbow room.

Through the gravel pit.

Up Bitch Hill. The Bitches are out there shaking tambourines.

Through the fish hatchery.

Rosy's field.

Last big hill … and you're on the lake.

Crossing the lake.

Wave at Grandpa's house.

Up main street.

Even five hours later, people are still cheering!

You make a final sprint for the benefit of the crowd.

You cross the line.

You're handed a massive medal, a beautiful medal that must weigh six pounds. Engraved on it is a picture of the original two skiers of the Norwegian Birkebeiner carrying the baby Haakonsson.

You undo your skis.

Off to find the bag of clothing you left at the drop-off point—hopefully it didn't get lost.

Change clothing.

You survived.

You made it.

You're part of the tradition now.

It feels indescribably good.

A warmth that can never be taken away.

Ever.

CHAPTER 13

Your first Birkie goes by in such a blur that you can't even process it. I was still reeling from the experience as we drove the Australians to the airport the following day. They had all finished the race somewhere between three and four hours. I couldn't understand how they could do it so fast.

At the gate, Kathryn gave me a hug and handed me a training diary.

"This is a vital piece of equipment for any skier," she said. "The elite guys do over five hundred hours a year."

"Then I'll do six hundred," I said.

She smiled. "In your first year you shouldn't do more than 250."

"That's for regular people. I'll shoot for 350."

That got her laughing.

"Maybe you can come down and ski our race, the Kangaroo Hoppet."

"Maybe."

And then they were gone.

On the way home, I picked up a pair of nylon wind pants. They weren't spandex tights, I still wasn't ready to wear those, but it was a step up from skiing in khakis.

It was a long, quiet ride back to the house.

Monday it was back to driving the dump truck and digging ditches at the cranberry marsh. At lunch, I dug out my Birkie medal to show everyone.

"This is what you get for skiing the Birkie."

They looked at it and handed it back.

"You can't hardly get through town on Birkie weekend," one of them said. "The roads are all jammed up."

That was the end of it. Sometimes the local color doesn't know what they've got going for them.

In April, I was listening to the radio at work when I heard the news that Kurt Cobain killed himself. My dad responded to the news by saying, "If I had Kurt Cobain's bank account, I'd be happy." To this day I don't know if that's true. When the lows get you, they can get you good.

I worked at the marsh through the summer and then quit.

I'd cleared about $15,000 at my job and, figuring oil would always be valuable, I dumped it all into energy stocks. I've made some bad choices in my life, but that wasn't one of them.

CHAPTER 14

I had some money and my spirits were higher so I decided to go back to college. I picked the University of Wisconsin-Stevens Point. I didn't even have a reason why I wanted to go there. Essentially, I went to Stevens Point because it wasn't Eau Claire and it wasn't Madison.

The greater part of my focus was on skiing and chatting with Kathryn. We quickly learned it was too expensive to call one another, so we took to writing letters and sending cassettes. I had my dorm room mostly to myself since my roommate showed up for the first two or three days then disappeared for the rest of the semester. He then showed up for finals and failed out of school. For the second semester, I had my own room.

When I had free time, I ran or I went to the gym. Doing something to better myself helped me relax. Somehow it was calming to feel I was making progress toward being a more complete person even if I didn't exactly see how all the pieces fit together. Sometimes the quest for self can be a perilous journey, and rather than think about it too much, you just need to put down your head and move forward. Anything that feels like a victory effectively is one.

Always, in the back of my mind, skiing nagged at me.

I thought of the elite-wave athletes, guys who could do the Birkie in around two hours. That was one-third of the time it took me. One-third!

I'd crossed the finish line exhausted. Where did they get the speed?

It seemed impossible.

Even the first wave seemed impossible, almost depressingly so.

But there was no giving up.

I resolved to see how good I could get. Even if I would never be any faster than a fifth-wave skier, I would be content with that. I didn't want anything to deter me.

All my life, I'd dealt with exercise-induced asthma. I never had attacks, but I started wheezing when I did any kind of physical activity. I always had one or two inhalers at close reach.

Despite having told my gym teacher of my asthma, he always gave me Cs. Actually, my asthma never really stopped me from participating, it was just that my gym teacher had decided I was a C student so he always gave me Cs. I didn't care much, except the frequent Cs kind of ruined my GPA. A secondary result that I had never been too aware of was that I'd gotten it pretty hardwired into me that I wasn't much of an athlete.

You've got to be careful about the untidy things that are floating around in your head. They can have an adverse effect on your entire life.

I resolved to disregard my PE teacher's evaluation and quit thinking of myself as physically average. I had to truly believe I could do more just to generate the ambition to give it a try.

There was a running trail behind the campus that went around a lake. It was a one-mile loop on a soft, chipped-wood surface. I'd go out there and run five or six miles and then take a rest on the bench that faced the lake.

Once after I finished a run, I walked to the bench and my old roommate was sitting there with a girl.

"Hey," he said tilting his head sideways, "you're my old roommate right?"

"Yup."

There was a brief silence.

"Are you ever coming back to school?" I asked.

"Nope."

"Well, good luck."

I ran home.

I never saw that guy again. Sometimes I wonder what happened to him.

CHAPTER 15

That summer after classes had ended, I met the guy who would turn out to be my main partner in crime during my skiing years. His name was Dean Franklin, and he was a big blond farm kid who looked more Nordic than Gunde Svan.

Dean's first love was bicycling, but it is nearly impossible to bicycle during a Wisconsin winter and Dean wanted something to help him stay in shape for those six or fifteen months. Skiing was a natural choice. However, it was summer when I met him, so we were in his domain. After a couple of weeks of riding together, he convinced me to do a bicycle race in his hometown.

It'd been a long time since I'd done a bicycle race. I'd gone through a period of racing when I was about thirteen and Greg LeMond's Tour de France victories were still clear in my mind. Most of the towns in Wisconsin have races on weekends. Church groups or others put them on as fund-raisers and a couple hundred people show up to test themselves. The skill level ranges from Category 1 U.S.C.F. racers to casual cyclists who are only out for a bit of exercise.

For those who have never seen a bike race, it's a pretty amazing sight.

At the sound of the gun, the pack leaps out from the gate, slowly disintegrating as weaker riders drop back and are left in the dust. The trick is to stay with the pack to shield yourself from the wind and maintain your speed. This technique is called drafting, but at thirteen, I had never stayed with the pack for more than a mile or two, so I wasn't familiar with how effective it can be. So as the day of Dean's hometown race approached, my expectations weren't very high.

I lined up toward the rear of the group, and when the gun fired, I did my best to stay with the pack, fully expecting to be peeled off in a matter of minutes. However, I soon found that your body does indeed develop substantially between the ages of thirteen and twenty. I was pleasantly surprised to discover it was actually not that difficult to stay up near the leaders.

I was just getting into a rhythm when up ahead I noticed Dean in his signature hunched-over style. He was riding a Fuji bicycle with a steel frame that visibly flexed under the pounding of his driving legs. It was probably the most inefficient combination of rider and bicycle out there, but he was nevertheless leading the pack of riders perched on thousand-dollar, replica professional team equipment.

About five miles into the race, I was tickled to still be in the lead group. On an impulse, I decided to catch up with Dean and say "Hi." I shifted down, pounded my legs, and moved my way through the pack, quickly finding that it was even more fun the closer you got to the front. It was raining slightly that day and the water on the road was causing greasy trails of brownish liquid to be thrown up by the bicycles' rear wheels. Getting up to the front got me out of the sprinkling lines of rooster tails.

I slid in alongside Dean with a big grin on my face. The grin meant to say, "Hey man, check this out, I'm still with the group even though I haven't been riding or racing all that much. Cool, huh?"

Dean turned to look at me with a mask of utter concentration and determination. The mud from the road had covered his fair features, and he looked like those guys on the old Tour de France posters from the age when they thought it was a good idea to light up a cigarette before they climbed a mountain because it helped "open the lungs."

At first I thought I detected annoyance in Dean's eyes as he recognized me, which was strange because Dean was about the most kind-hearted person I'd ever met. In fact, Dean is so kind-hearted that the only time I have ever seen him angry was during a trip to Colorado when I accidentally lit the gas can he was holding on fire. Even then, he only stayed mad for a couple of hours, and after the skin grafts, you couldn't even tell there had ever been an incident.

But races change the hearts of men, and in the thick of them, even close friends become foes and rivals. Unless, of course, they can be used to create the winning break-away.

An instant after seeing me, the annoyance evaporated, and Dean signaled with a sharp, forward pointing motion with his hand. He then sprinted ahead of the main group.

Sprinting ahead was the last thing I wanted to do, but Dean had given me no other choice. I couldn't very well leave my friend out there alone in the front without at least putting up the pretense of going with him. So, even though I thought it was going to ruin my chances of staying with the pack until the finish, I gallantly sprinted to join Dean in his inspired break-away five miles into the race.

There was never any doubt in my mind that it was a fool's charge, but it was still exhilarating. I caught up to Dean's wheel and hunkered down to conserve as much energy as I could and get out of the wind. The brownish water from the road sprayed off of Dean's rear wheel into my squinting, blinking eyes. It was glorious!

Dean's acceleration was phenomenal. He quickly pushed us up from twenty-five to twenty-eight miles an hour. The pack shrank behind us as we flew down the wet asphalt.

"We've got a gap!" Dean cried. Oh, how I wished that I had been a strong bicycle racer and that we could have taken that break away all the way to the finish line. But as my adrenaline rush started to wear off, I realized how much trouble I was having keeping up with my companion.

"OK," he said, "pull through."

Shoot! Now it was up to me. As Dean pulled off to the side, I put my head down and drove into the wind. Dean slipped in behind me to take a well-earned rest on my churning wheel and I continued to pound my legs with as much force as I could muster. The countryside flew by. My breath came in ragged spurts, the rain turned into a torrential downpour and the heavens broke open in a cataclysmic eruption. No matter what the outcome of the day, at that moment, I was in the lead. It was a great feeling.

For a while, it seemed like I was maintaining the gap that Dean had created. Then we hit a hill and the wind was knocked out of me. In an instant, the pack was around us again, and I slipped into the back of the group where I could do no further damage to Dean's aspirations or tactics.

I did manage to stay with the pack until the very end, and finished in the top twenty or so. Dean wasn't happy because he hadn't won, but the fact that I had been leading for a while was enough to make the day a success for me. I'd done far better than I'd thought possible, so naturally I decided that if I kept training I would one day win the Tour de France or an Olympic gold medal or something.

It's good to have lofty goals. Life's short, why aim low?

CHAPTER 16

As summer faded into fall, I decided it was time for me to get serious about skiing and make myself a waxing bench.

Cross-country skiing isn't so much a sport as it is an art form. It isn't so much a hobby as it is a way of life. Like all hobbies, the more committed to it you become, the crazier the peripheral objects—and people—you start dealing with.

Just like with any sport, the object of cross-country skiing is to go fast.

Theoretically, skis go fast because the bases compress the snow into a bead of water. This happens at the microscopic level so don't expect to see rivers flowing out from beneath your skis. The ski creates just enough liquid to slip on and glides along on this bead. It's kind of the same idea as the Egyptian slaves who pushed massive stone blocks around on rolling logs. But in the case of the slaves, somebody always had to pick up the logs behind the block and run them back to the front—skis just compress new beads of water as they go.

Waxing is the process by which cross-country skiers apply a base layer to their skis to make them faster under various conditions. They literally use wax, but not the beeswax you find in candles. The wax skiers use is a chemically formulated product jam-packed with water-repelling compounds like "fluorocarbons"—whatever those are. The only technical detail I have about them is that they're really expensive.

Base preparation is where skiing turns into alchemy and good ski waxers turn into folk heroes.

If you think an Eskimo has a large vocabulary of words that mean "snow," you've never talked to a cross-country skier.

Skiers will go on and on about the never-ending varieties of snow.

New snow.

Old snow.

Wet snow.

Dry snow.

Abrasive snow.

Soft snow.

The list is endless.

And for every one of these snow types there is a different wax. Additionally, there is a variation with how the snow reacts depending on the day's temperature, so there are different waxes for different snow types and different temperatures. Then you have to keep in mind that the temperature is not going to stay consistent throughout the day, so you have to make the choice of whether you want to have fast skis at the beginning of the race, or if you want to wax for the conditions you anticipate will exist at the end of the race. This is a tricky proposition, but if you're doing a marathon distance and you notice that your skis are getting faster as you become more and more exhausted, it provides a mental edge that's hard to beat.

Yes, wax is important, although there are those in the cross-country skiing world who say waxing is secondary to the structure of your skis' bases. These people have a variety of tools at their disposal, ranging from a ten-dollar hand-held riller tool to a fifty-thousand-dollar stone-grinder machine, used for putting various cross-hatch or line patterns onto the bases of their skis.

As you can imagine, it is within waxing mythology that the cross-country skiing business is founded.

It can be overwhelming when you're just starting out.

But the fact is that as a new skier you don't have to be overly concerned with wax, just like you don't have to be overly concerned with presenting algebra to your newborn baby—there's time for the evolution. If you're just getting into skiing, simply slap a couple boards on your feet and enjoy the winter wonderland. It's only when you start doing marathons that you begin wanting to know how to get faster with the same effort.

If you ever wondered where elite skiers get their speed, a lot of it is due to conditioning. But at least part of it is due to superior waxing.

Well, swimming as I was in this sea of confusion and expense, I decided that before I started applying myself to achieving a doctorate in waxing, I needed a simple wax bench. The bench stabilizes your skis as you apply, scrape and brush the wax. It's almost like you're taking your skis to a fancy spa as a bribe, you have to pamper them like crazy before they'll be willing to carry you for miles and miles at breakneck speeds.

As you can imagine, every ski shop in the universe is only too happy to sell you a wax bench. However, I didn't feel like spending any money. Instead of buying a bench, I went down to our garage and found an old two-by-six that had been sitting in the corner since before the beginning of time. I laid this on its side and placed a 210-centimeter cross-country ski on it and traced its outline. Then, I cut along the outline with a jigsaw, taking an extra rectangular piece out in the middle of the board to make room for the binding. I slapped a couple pieces of wood on either side with a couple bolts and wing-nuts to make a crude latching device, and voila, I had a wax bench that looked like something the Vikings might have used to cross the Atlantic.

"Real" skiers would come to my house and look at my bench and wrinkle their noses.

"What … is … that … ?" they'd ask, their voices dripping ill-concealed disdain.

"A wax bench … try it!"

And they'd try it and become converted.

The darn thing worked like a charm!

Twenty years later, it's still in daily use during ski season.

CHAPTER 17

F all continued on its merry way, and Dean and I started to feel ready to get off the dry land and onto some snow. Skiers are a funny bunch in that they rejoice at a forecast calling for the white stuff, rather than cringe in disgust like regular people do. Dean and I took to huddling around the radio searching random stations far and wide in the hope that winter flakes had been seen or reported somewhere.

After several weeks of searching, we finally got a hot tip that the town of Ironwood, Michigan, sometimes was the beneficiary—not the term the residents would have used—of "lake-effect" snow.

Lake-effect snow is caused pretty much by the presence of Lake Superior. Frankly, you can't just dump thousands of gallons of water in the middle of the Northwoods like that and not expect it to have some sort of effect on the surrounding territory. The result of lake-effect snow is that all the areas within a certain distance of Lake Superior get snow before everyone else. Oddly, of all the areas in the region, it seems like Ironwood, Michigan, gets hit harder than anywhere else.

We were innocently sitting around, desperately surfing the airwaves one afternoon, when we perked up at the sound of a crackly voice telling us that snow had fallen on Ironwood.

"How much snow?" we asked, looking at each other with excitement.

The voice garbled on, fading into static as if the speaker's broadcast center had just been overwhelmed by a terrible blizzard consuming the area in meters of fluffy white stuff.

"What do you think?" Dean asked me.

"I think we should head up there!" I replied. "There are obviously massive snowbanks clogging up the streets of Ironwood."

We looked at the clock—it was already four in the afternoon.

Now, any reasonable skier knows that you can't go hellbent for leather at the first hint of a rumor of snow. Even if there was enough snow to ski on, the trails would still have to be groomed and prepared. You simply can't just jump in your car and head out and think you're going to have a wonderful skiing adventure.

However, none of that was the point for us back then. We were just excited about the prospect of snow. It intoxicated us, frankly. If there was even the smallest chance of snow, we had to get out there and ski.

We called some of our friends.

"Have you heard that there's snow in Ironwood?"

"Where did you hear that?

"We didn't hear it exactly … we more or less inferred it from the radio. We're heading up there now though, want to come?"

"You guys are crazy!"

Click.

But their lack of enthusiasm didn't dampen ours, and before long we were piling into my ridiculous Chevy Blazer that consumed fifty-seven gallons of gasoline per mile and speeding crazily toward Ironwood.

The trail from Twin Pines, Wisconsin, to Ironwood, Michigan, would become overly familiar to us during the next few years as Ironwood would always have snow before anyone else. In time, a great little ski facility named ABR— active backwoods retreat—would appear and become the "it" training destination for skiers in the early season. However, ABR did not yet exist and Dean and I were going to have to make do skiing on a golf course or something. It wasn't as good as skiing on a groomed trail, but if you were jonesing for some snow time, you could pack down your own trail by skiing in circles. It worked well enough and it gave you a heck of a workout.

The Blazer bounced down the highway. That car didn't roll, it bounced. Chevrolet Blazers are great for pulling boats, but they're no darn good at cornering.

The sun was dropping fast and the sheer craziness of our escapade hadn't escaped us entirely but we weren't about to allow our spirits to be dampened. I decided that we needed to get there fast.

"How long does it usually take to get to Ironwood?" I asked Dean casually.

"At 2:15 or so, why do you ask?"

"Because I'm going to set the record!"

I hit the gas.

The Blazer tore up Highway GG. Highway GG is a curvy little road with deer, possum and all other forms of wildlife just waiting around every turn to jump out and explode into red mist before the terrible charging power of my Chevy Blazer. As we bounded along the highway, we gazed out with keen and terrified eyes for any sign of wildlife or traffic authorities that might be lying in wait to totally wreck our day.

But luck was with us, and after only suffering one or two scares in which we really thought that Blazer was going to roll over, go tumbling into a swamp, and explode into flames, we pulled into Ironwood in a record time of 1:39 that, to my knowledge, still stands to this day.

It was already pretty dark as we stood in the middle of that desolate little town, but we were in heaven because the landscape was blanketed in a soft and twinkling white powder.

There was snow everywhere.

We had seen signs of snow for the last fifteen minutes on the road, but we hadn't been prepared for what awaited us at Ironwood. The ground was buried beneath a good four or five inches of accumulation.

We were psyched!

"Where do we go now?" Dean asked.

"Let's find a park or something where we can ski ourselves a track!"

We drove around town looking for a park. The snow was hard-packed on the street and we had to adopt the slick-surface driving techniques known to all residents of hard winter climates. In a little while we found a small park.

"Hooray!" we cried, slapping on our ski gear and leaping out into the very mouth of insanity.

I put my skis on the brand new, twinkling white surface.

I pushed forward, expecting my ski to glide along as it always did.

Instead, it came to a jerking halt and I nearly fell over.

"What the heck?" I said, trying again.

Typically there is a certain resistance when you try to ski on fresh snow, but it usually goes away when the snow is compacted into a hard surface. The principle is the same as when you crush a handful of fluffy powder into a snowball. It compresses into a block of ice.

But this snow didn't compact. Worse, it piled up and stuck to the base of the ski.

"I've never seen this before!" Dean said.

We clomped around and did everything we could, but the snow simply wouldn't pack for us. Some unusual combination of snow temperature and air temperature was creating conditions that made trail packing impossible. We even tried stomping out a track just by walking and then skiing over it, but the second we put our skis to the compressed snow, the snow just clamped onto our bases and left long green patches of grass exposed to the night as we stumbled around frantically.

"This is so weird!" I cried.

For a moment, our spirits were dampened. The ridiculous drive up to the middle of nowhere now seemed to have been a disheartening waste of time. Our theory was that the ground was simply too warm to allow the snow to pack up right. It wasn't like the permafrost you get later in the year. The lake-effect snow was an anomaly, so it only made sense that it would act like an anomaly when you skied on it.

After about half an hour, we finally had to admit that it was going to be impossible to pack down a track and ski. We looked at each other dejectedly.

"Well … what now?"

About then, we noticed a vehicle passing by on the roads. It was moving slowly as it slipped and slid along the packed and icy surface.

"I know," I said. "Let's ski on the roads!"

Dean looked down at his skis. Like me, he was using an old pair of skis that he had designated as "rock skis." You use your rock skis early in the season before there is a good base of snow. This is because before you have a good base, rocks, twigs, and other obstructions can still poke through the trail and ruin the bottoms of your skis as you pass over them.

"Why not?" he said.

Carefully we hiked over to the road, clipped our skis into our boots and took off.

It worked like a charm.

There we were, sprinting along on our skis down the streets of Ironwood. Occasionally, cars would pass us with an annoyed honk, but we didn't care. We were enjoying the absurdity of the moment. For about two solid hours we skied, exploring the strange trail of the city street that would, in all likelihood, never be available for our skiing enjoyment again.

At last, euphoric and exhausted, we climbed back into my vehicle and headed home. The instant we arrived, we had to call everyone and tell them how awesome it was. I've found that it's better in life to always claim your exploits were awesome, regardless of whether or not they actually were.

"We were the first on snow this year," Dean said.

Being the first on snow for a season is always a nice bragging right to have.

CHAPTER 18

I was feeling better about life in general by the time my second Birkie rolled around, and physically I was far better prepared for the event. True to my word, I'd kept track of my training throughout the year and accumulated more than three hundred hours of ski-specific training. I felt confident for the upcoming Birkie.

Although three hundred hours might seem like a lot, it's actually very little compared to what top athletes do throughout a year. Just to be clear, an hour of training doesn't mean you have to sprint at top speed for the full sixty minutes. It's acceptable to jog at a leisurely pace, or even a fast walk if you're just starting out. The point of keeping a training journal is simply to orient yourself in your own program and to help you maximize the results you get from your efforts.

The journal helps motivate you to exercise, and gives you some pride in your achievement beyond what can be obtained from race results. But it doesn't have to be at all complicated or difficult. Really, when you're just starting out, the whole object of a training run is to just not slow down to a walk during your session. The definition of running is that at some point during your stride both of your feet have to leave contact with the ground, but this doesn't have to be a leap—a simple little hop works quite well. Trust me when I tell you there are a lot of speeds in between your slowest and your fastest running pace. If you're really good, you can even run or jog more slowly than you walk.

Kathryn called the slow sessions "LSD" sessions, like the hallucinogen. But in this case, LSD doesn't stand for Lysergic Acid Diethylamide but Long, Slow Distance— that's the problem with acronyms, they're ambiguous. Essentially eighty percent of your training should be LSD training. It's only in that last twenty percent that you do strenuous activities like weight lifting, some interval runs, or race-pace training. The trick is to make all of your training sessions fun, to mix them up so they don't become boring. For example, you could play a two-hour game of basketball once a week to fulfill your strenuous exercise quota.

The challenge of designing a yearly exercise plan is to discover something that's sustainable. If you punish yourself too much, you just aren't going to stick to the plan. Once you get into the routine—like brushing your teeth—training becomes part of your life.

So I went into my second Birkie with a lot more confidence than the previous year. First of all, I knew I could complete the event—I'd survived the previous year on much less preparation. Second, I knew the course better. Third, I had started wearing high-tech clothing. I wasn't one of those Lycra guys yet, but I did have some puffy black track pants that did a better job of keeping the water off me than my old khaki pants did. In addition, I'd abandoned my wool button-up shirt for a cotton T-shirt with a portrait of Dostoevsky on the chest. Cotton's not the ideal fabric for wearing outdoors, so I had a good polypro against my skin, but on the outside it was big Fyodor. I bet I'm the only guy who has ever skied the Birkie while wearing a Fyodor Dostoevsky T-shirt. I don't know why I made that choice exactly, I suppose I just thought it was funny.

As the Birkie approached, the yearly contingent of international skiers again began to trickle into my neck of the woods. I was excited to have my Australian friends return, and the moment they did, we found any and every excuse we could to go and hang out with my crazy grandpa. We used to stop at his place for a cup of coffee or tea after a long ski on the Birkie trail, and he'd regale us with one story after another of different times, different places, and different ways of perceiving the world.

The ski season went by in a rush and before we knew it, we were again making the long drive to Telemark to pick up our Birkie bibs. On the return trip, we stopped to visit Grandpa, who was only too happy to tell us a story about something that happened when he was a military doctor back in World War II.

"You know, we used to get a good viral strain going that we wanted to keep around for giving inoculations."

"What kind of strain?"

"Oh … you know, small pox, bubonic plague, malaria," he said with a wave of his hands, "any kind of thing the soldiers might get into and the generals wanted available vaccinations for."

He'd intermittently start to cough and giggle as he told the story. He might interrupt himself in this fashion for five full minutes, but nobody ever dared start a different anecdote When Grandpa held the floor, he was in charge.

"Well, there'd be times when we'd get a good strain going and we'd keep it alive in the patients. But when all the patients got better or needed to be discharged, we'd lose the strain. So what we used to do is … we'd go outside and get a hobo or something and tell him he could come and sleep in the hospital for a while. Then we'd inject him with our malaria strain, so that we'd have it on the premises … hehehe!"

As he said this, the hilarity of using a hard-on-his-luck human being for an incubator just overtook him and he almost collapsed in laughter.

We all sat there watching him with the same horrified expressions we had when he taught us how not to drive on black ice.

It's amazing how people born as little as fifty years ago come from a completely different era. Or maybe it was a complete fabrication and he was just trying to shock us. Then again, maybe it was just Grandpa being Grandpa.

You never know.

CHAPTER 19

The emotion of my second Birkie was like a magnified version of the first. Having done the race before, I knew what to expect and didn't feel the same anxiety of newness. The whole Birkie experience had gone by so fast the prior year that I had hardly even been able to admire its passing. For my second Birkie, however, it was as if the event had slowed down. I was able to focus on simply absorbing the ambiance, which only served to make the whole experience all the more amazing.

Again, we rode the buses at four-thirty in the morning. Again, we waited desperately at the start for the race to begin, stomping our feet to overcome the cold and making silly jokes to overcome our nerves. I'd moved from the eighth to the sixth wave so I was going earlier than the year before.

The gun went off, and I was transported to that magical world that only exists once a year between the starting line in Cable and the finish line in Hayward. I was skiing the Birkie with thousands of other mad winter sport enthusiasts. There is always a special energy on Birkie day, a collective high that all the skiers create and experience together.

Right away I could feel that my form was better. Bit by bit, little by little, I was learning how to ski and my body was adapting to the task.

This year, I had my own skis. I'd finally bought a pair of Fischers. They glided beneath me like heavenly chariots. The snow felt like a cloud.

I was skiing.

On a fast day, skiing is as close to flying under your own power as you can get.

The course sighed and unfurled beneath me.

And then it started to climb and the illusion of flight was replaced with cold, hard work.

The hills!

The hills in the Birkie are unmatched by any other course in the region. You might do a ten-kilometer race or two in Wisconsin or Minnesota to prepare for the Birkie, but nothing prepares you for it as well as the actual Birkie course.

The Birkie hills climb endlessly. They drag agonizingly on and knead the breakfast from your belly as they repeatedly throttle you in a wrestler's choke.

It's funny, but the hills are so distinct on the Birkie trail that they have developed individual personalities. It takes very little description for people who have skied the Birkie to know which infamous climb you are talking about.

To start, there are the power lines. A cruel series of inclines at the beginning of the race that are like an endless stairway to the house of the gods. In the starting kilometers of the race, you're skiing in the cleared-out area beneath the power lines of Northern Wisconsin. The never ending sequence of hills is exceptionally steep and abrupt. At one or two points, there is a choice of trails to take as the groomed path diverts around the power pole itself. Don't be fooled, there is no "easier" path, except possibly the path that seems harder before you actually end up making a choice.

At the end of the power lines, you turn left and head into the woods. Now you've got an eight- to ten-kilometer climb to the top of the divide and the high point of the trail. As the course winds through the woods, there are two or three memorable hills. One is a downhill that curves sharply to the left and is usually littered with snowmobilers who have come to mock the athletes as they stumble through the rutted course. This is the first of two points along the trail where the snowmobile gangs accumulate. The second is beyond the divide just north of Highway OO and has come to be known as Heckler's Hill. They stand on the sidelines and cheer as racers lose their balance in the choppy terrain or dive out of the way to avoid crashing competitors.

As you're climbing the divide, you don't have energy to waste worrying about snowmobilers or Heckler's Hill. The divide captures all of your attention. It's like a reposing dragon that stretches from the start of the race to the trail's high point. Climbing the final hill is like scurrying up the neck of the beast and stomping on its head. The hill just before the high point is a brutal monster. It sucks the last whiff of willpower you'd been hoarding in anticipation of a moment of weakness. You ski out of an overhung forest trail to the base of the mountain, where the shadows seem to part out of deference to the mountain's stark and endless pitch.

Even if you struggle to the top, the divide beats you. It is one of those hills that appears to be a certain height and then folds out again at the false summit to reveal you still have half the climb to go. Most of the time you spend the entire ascent recalculating how fast you can finish the Birkie.

At the top, there is a small sign that says "High Point of the Trail," but you have no energy to celebrate. The only thing that keeps you going is the knowledge that immediately after the divide you are treated to about five kilometers of trail that is predominantly downhill.

But even that respite is small comfort, for the seasoned Birkie veteran knows the divide hill has three malicious children laying in wait along the remainder of the course. No, they're not quite as terrible as their unyielding mother, but they remind you of her and they make you shudder in agony.

The first is about five kilometers north of OO. It is a curvy serpent of a climb just before Boedecker road. My mom started calling it "green man hill" because she once saw a guy on that hill who was turning green. Whether he was green from illness, over-exertion, dehydration, or some combination of the three, nobody can say, but, for me, the name stuck.

There are a couple more bumps on the way in to OO and then you're free for a long stretch, until you go down, down, down almost to the end of the race. Down to a mere ten kilometers, when you run into the infamous Bitch Hill.

Bitch Hill is arguably the toughest individual hill on the trail, but its location on the course is what really makes it a killer. You're eighty percent done with the race when you stumble to the foot of Bitch Hill, which means you're also eighty percent spent.

Bitch Hill is the Heartbreak Hill of the Birkie.

Bitch Hill is the Birkie's L'alpe d'Huez.

Like the final hill of the Divide, Bitch Hill starts steep and hard and when you think you've reached the summit, it reveals cruelly that your climb has only just begun.

Generally there are spectators from Hayward there to help you along. They aren't malicious like the various snowmobilers along the course. No, these people have come out to encourage you. On Bitch Hill, they disguise themselves as bitches. Men and women alike. This generally means there are a lot of false wigs and various other false attributes of one kind or another. Strange things pass for humor when you're in the midst of a white-land marathon in subfreezing conditions.

At the top of Bitch Hill, you start a blissful three-kilometer run of essentially downhill trail. This is where you make up the time you lost climbing that foul banshee.

After Bitch Hill, you continue toward the fish hatchery. There's a big hill right before the fish hatchery parking area but it's not one of the major hills, although it misses out on this distinction by just a hair. Then you're skiing down, up, down again into Rosie's field where the race, as well as the Pre-Birkie, has started on more than one occasion.

You cross Highway 77 only to find yourself at the foot of another monster. It's a series of monsters actually, but somehow, though these hills are probably bigger and meaner than even Bitch Hill, they aren't so intimidating. You're at the end of the race now, it's just a matter of putting your head down and gutting it out.

Up, up, up you go. The hills fall out and continue stacking upon themselves. You heave. You push. You rise toward the heavens, and just when you think you can't take anymore, the sky breaks to the realization that you're finally done climbing.

Now it's down.

Down to Lake Hayward and the last crossing. A couple kilometers on the perfectly flat surface of the lake. With every stride, you see Main Street growing. You hear the roar of the crowd, the tin microphone of the announcer saying names.

"Bob Highlands from Mendoza ... "

"Katie Swift from Seeley ... "

"Ethan Shattuck from Twin Pines ... "

The names keep ticking off, and although you're in a

daze, and you're ready to collapse, you know you have to keep going until you hear them call your name.

"Arthur Miller from Duluth … "

"Kyle Mackey from Trego … "

"Melissa Heavers from Superior … "

Up Main Street you go, through the bells and the whistles. The people cheer for you like you're about to be bequeathed with an olive wreath. They're ringing bells, drinking beer, occasionally one of them recognizes you and calls out encouragement, but you don't acknowledge it. You have a task to finish. The Birkie needs to be finished.

With a couple more strides you're there.

Your name is called.

Somebody clips your Birkie pin to your bib so you won't lose it in the chaos.

Somebody else unclips your skis from your feet.

You stumble over to get your gear bag.

You have a few minutes before the sweat on your body turns to ice. But in those first few seconds of finishing the event, you're still a furnace, and you can strip down to your bare chest, heedless of the elements.

The Birkie!

It's an eternal day that's over all too briefly.

CHAPTER 20

Finishing the Birkie is an amazing achievement. It's something that nobody can ever take away. Sometimes people get too caught up in the concept of winning and losing to truly appreciate the entirety of the Birkie experience. When you're sitting at home watching TV, I guess it is relevant who wins and who loses since you need some sort of visual hook to stop you from changing the channel.

Frankly, I don't care much about the people on TV. I'm far more interested in having my own adventures instead of sitting around watching somebody else have theirs.

There are some people who will laugh at you for dedicating a huge amount of your time to a sporting event that you will never have a realistic chance of winning.

But you don't ski the Birkie for its sake, you ski it for yours.

Some people like to say that everyone who skis the Birkie or does a marathon is a winner, but even that is a little too wishy-washy for me. I don't like to put it in terms of "winning" and have "winning" be the only positive word that comes out of doing a race.

It's much bigger than that.

When you do the Birkie, you learn something about yourself.

Now, you'd think that, due to the fact that you live with yourself 24 hours a day, you'd know everything about yourself there is to know.

This isn't true.

The fact is, at a fairly early age, you get into a routine.

For most people this is a comfortable routine.

This is a safe routine.

Your routine is a controlled environment, and chances are you've chosen that routine because you know you'll be able to handle everything that confronts you on any given day. You get up, go to work, come home, watch *American Idol*, eat dinner, brush your teeth, and go to bed (repeated endlessly).

It's the "easy" track at the go-kart rink.

It's the bunny hill at the ski slopes.

In contrast, when you're in a ski race, you're in control of nothing.

People shoot by you on hills and demonstrate a degree of discipline and athleticism that you didn't believe was possible.

The trail will kick and tumble beneath you and make you realize the world is not static or stable.

You'll reach a point of exhaustion where you will have to look deep inside yourself and decide whether or not you truly have the reserves or the willpower to make yourself continue.

Not everybody who does the Birkie "wins."

Some of them discover weaknesses within their character and within their bodies they might have preferred never to have come to light.

But once these weaknesses are revealed, you have two choices.

You can go back to how you lived before and pretend they aren't there.

Or you can overcome them.

It doesn't matter where you are on the social ladder—the Birkie tests everyone equally and without bias. A billionaire will never know how precious and beautiful an orange tastes after fifty kilometers of skiing unless he or she skis fifty kilometers and eats one.

The particular taste of that orange doesn't exist anywhere in reality except at the end of an extreme effort.

You can't buy it.

You can't hire somebody to go and get it for you.

You have to achieve it yourself.

And if you do achieve it, you will be rewarded.

Guaranteed.

In a world filled with artificial colors and sweeteners, the Birkie is a vibrant swath of blissful, primordial reality.

I'd finished my second Birkie an hour faster than my first and was overjoyed with the result. I'd also moved from the sixth wave to the fourth, steadily progressing up the ladder. In the distance, the first and elite waves still hovered like a distant mirage. They seemed unattainable, but I was closer now.

I resolved to increase my training to four hundred hours for the upcoming year.

In my quest to find other goals to quell my Birkie fever in the lean summer months, I stumbled across a magazine ad for a running race in Duluth, Minnesota.

"Grandma's Marathon," 26.2 miles.

I'd never done a running race in my life.

Without another thought, I filled in the entry form and sent in the check before the logical part of my brain could stop me.

CHAPTER 21

Considering that I had a marathon to prepare for, I decided that I'd better start training. In my typical fashion, I didn't bother to read any books or do any Internet searches to find out what the best way of preparing for a marathon is. Had I done so, I would have probably found all kinds of three-month plans in which you do a series of training runs that steadily increase in length and that culminate in about a twenty-miler a few weeks before the official event. There are people who swear by doing a regimented, tried and true plan like that.

I'm not one of those people.

I'm more of the "jump in the deep end without looking and see how much trouble you get into" type of guy. I was young and fit back then and I could get away with that kind of foolishness.

I'd done quite a bit of running the previous year for ski training, even though I hadn't really liked it. But I'd done it anyway because it's a good way to get in shape for cross-country skiing. Back when I was going to school in Stevens Point, I used to run loops around the one-mile lake that was near the campus.

The good thing about running is that you don't need to go anywhere special to do it. If you need a quick workout, just slap on your shoes and head out the door. It's convenient, it's easy, and it can beat you into the ground.

I was only running about three or four hours a week, tossing in the occasional two-hour "endurance" run for good measure.

About a month before Grandma's, there was a nice little race in Grantsberg, Wisconsin, called the Syttende Mai—Norwegian for May 17—to celebrate Norwegian Independence day. A lot of the little towns in Wisconsin have festivals like this to celebrate their founders' heritage. I've picked up a lot of fun trivia facts doing events like this, although I keep waiting for the words Syttende Mai to show up on Jeopardy.

The race was 16.2 miles—they don't run it anymore as far as I know—which was a good distance because, if you were doing a marathon, you'd only have 10 miles left to go. Grantsberg had planned it that way so people would be enticed to do the event to train for Grandma's.

My crazy training for my first running marathon sort of mirrored my crazy training for my first Birkie. For that, I did the pre-Birkie, a long ski, and the actual event. For Grandma's it was the Syttende Mai, a long run, and the marathon.

I can't remember my time at the Syttende Mai, but I suffered enough that I figured I'd better cram in some emergency training in the few weeks left before the run. About a week and a half before Grandma's, I left my house for what was to be a four-hour training run. Of course it was too hot and I didn't bring any water and I ended up more or less walking back to the house where I collapsed, exhausted, under a cool shower for about a day and a half and seriously rethought just what I'd gotten myself into.

But there was no going back.

I'd paid the entry fee, after all.

As the last few days before the run dried up, I dialed back my running almost to zero. In contrast, my anxiety ratcheted as high as it could go.

But there was no backing out.

***

We got a reservation in a dorm room up in Duluth for the night of the race. My mom came along to watch because she more or less thought I was committing suicide. She's usually pretty intrepid about following me along on crazy adventures, but to this day she's never done a marathon, probably because she's borne witness to the sorry state in which those darn things leave me.

The dorm room was miserable, of course, but you don't sleep all that well the night before your first marathon. I was up all night in the bathroom because I thought it was a good idea to hydrate by drinking an entire gallon of Gatorade. People frequently laugh at my Gatorade addiction, but when I tell them that I've never once had a cramp in my entire life … ever … they usually quiet right down.

By the time my alarm went off at the fiendish hour of three or four in the morning, I was too wired to stay in bed any longer anyway.

I'd done exactly thirty hours of running in preparation for Grandma's.

I was counting on thirty hours of running for the months of April, May, and the beginning of June, in addition to whatever fitness had carried over from the ski season to get me through the marathon. Although I'd supplemented that with some bicycling and weight room work, any athlete will tell you that thirty hours of training in three months is pretty light.

But I was young ... so I was too dumb to care.

However, I was smart enough to be anxious.

What I lacked in training, I made up for in other ways. I'd applied my deductive reasoning to the marathon chafing problem.

In case you didn't know, running a marathon is hard on a body in more ways than just physical exhaustion and dehydration. You also have to consider the toll rubbing fabric has on your body.

If you've ever watched a marathon, you'll see guys come running in with parallel red stains on the front of their lightweight racing singlet. Although those singlets are as flimsy as a tissue, their weight and friction of movement over the course of 26.2 miles causes the fibers to dig deep into the soft tissues you find on a person's body.

In other words—running a marathon makes your nipples bleed.

And that's not to mention what it does to your feet, your thighs, and even the places where your shorts come in contact with your waist.

Any area of friction is going to be rubbed raw.

For some reason, I'd considered this. I'm not sure if somebody told me or if I just got lucky, but I'd made darn sure to bring a whole tub of petroleum jelly up to the race to lube myself up with.

My philosophy was that if you could put oil and grease into a car to stop the grinding, you could certainly put some on a human body to stop the chafing.

That morning, when my alarm went off, I jumped into the shower to be fresh and renewed before the event. Still dripping wet, I sat on the little dorm bed and applied a generous amount of petroleum jelly to every single crevice on my body that I could easily reach—I even went after a few that were a bit of a stretch. Let me tell you, I didn't skimp on that stuff either. I had big wads of petroleum jelly hanging everywhere, with the largest globs going on my feet, between my toes and on my heels.

Shorts, socks, and shoes never had an easier time slipping onto a man's body.

Number in place, I jumped on the bus, rode to the start and looked around at all the people. Under my breath, I spoke these prophetic words:

"I'm going to die!"

But about then the gun went off and there was nothing else to think about but to run, run, run.

Five steps into the race, I realized that, like the Birkie, this was a special event.

There I was again in marathon time … that time of life that only exists while you're in the midst of some massive, ridiculous sporting event.

Reality is skewed.

You see things more clearly.

The world is brighter and better.

For some reason, the self-imposed pressure to perform well was completely off at Grandma's marathon that year. I just trotted along the north shore of Lake Superior like everyone else, enjoying the warm summer day and chit-chatting with people who were just as disgusted with themselves as I was for doing something as absurd as a marathon.

Yet there we were.

And at the finish line again lay an understanding that couldn't be bought.

As I ran, I made sure I drank a lot of water

I made sure I ate a lot of oranges.

I kept my spirits up.

And four hours and twenty minutes later, I was standing at the finish line wearing my brand-new marathon completion medal. They funneled us through a chute that ended in something akin to a doctor's office. There were people there to shine lights in my eyes to make sure I was still conscious or something. I pretty much bowed to their will since I didn't have the strength to fight it. Never had I felt such a physical exhaustion. My legs were completely gone, they'd been shaken and pounded into pulp from the pavement. My lungs burned, and I was covered with a thick sheen that was a mixture of sweat and the water that I'd been dumping on my head throughout the race. All of this had coagulated on my body like embryonic fluid, and standing there at the finish line, it was almost like being reborn.

About then, a volunteer wrapped me in a space blanket. I was so broken down and vulnerable that I started to shiver even in the midday heat, but it was glorious because I felt as if I was ready to start building myself back up to someone stronger and better than before.

One more little piece of my identity had been revealed and snapped into place.

One more thing had been struck off the bucket list.

Becoming a marathoner is no small club to be a part of.

Before I even really thought about it, I knew I'd be putting that event on my calendar for the subsequent year.

CHAPTER 22

I'd been saving my money from before Grandma's marathon because I was planning to head to Australia to ski the Kangaroo Hoppet, the Australian entry on the Worldloppet tour. Ever since I'd started hanging out at ski races, the rumor of the Worldloppet tour had been whispering on the wind, and I had been itching with curiosity to find out more about it.

The Worldloppet is a series of ski races that stretches the globe. The races have been around for a long time, but again it was Tony Wise who was instrumental in connecting them in an international series. Each of the races on the Worldloppet circuit has a unique personality, and there are currently fifteen Worldloppet races. For example, the Birkie is the event for the U.S. The Gatineau Loppet—formerly the Keskinada—is the event in Canada and the Marcialonga— the "long march"—is the event in Italy.

After each race, points are awarded to the top thirty male and top thirty female finishers. At the end of the season, the skier with the most points is crowned champion.

The Worldloppet series is a tremendous event for elite

skiers, but it also has great appeal for amateur skiers like me. Anyone can become a Worldloppet member for a small fee. The membership certificate is a passport with a list of all the Worldloppet events. Skiers who complete ten of the fifteen races qualify as a Worldloppet master and their names are recorded with all the other Worldloppet masters on the Worldloppet webpage and in various publications. There is no time requirement for completing your passport, so, like cross-country skiing in general, it's a lifetime undertaking.

As you can probably tell, becoming a Worldloppet master brings with it a hefty amount of bragging rights. To complete your passport means that not only have you done ten world-class marathon events, but you've done them in ten different countries. The logistics and expense involved, not to mention the training and physical fitness requirements, make the completion of the series a daunting commitment. In fact, many avid skiers find they can't complete their passport until after they retire. But the difficulties are what make the Worldloppet circuit so special. Traveling from country to country in pursuit of marathon ski races is a heck of a way to see the world.

I was under no illusions that I'd be completing my Worldloppet passport anytime soon, but I resolved to take advantage of any opportunity to do a Worldloppet race whenever one presented itself. I had a standing invitation to come to Australia from my Birkie friends, so my plan was to jump on a plane the day after Grandma's marathon and head on down to Melbourne to race the Kangaroo

Hoppet. I had my newly purchased Worldloppet passport in hand and was excited about getting my first international stamp.

As you can imagine, my emotions were running high. However, as the travel date approached circumstances conspired to separate me from my US Passport, which put the prospect of my trip in jeopardy.

Being separated from your passport is never an agreeable experience, but it's especially unsettling when it happens on the cusp of a trip of a lifetime. To make matters worse, I had no one but myself to blame for my dire circumstances as you will shortly see.

Back then, you needed a visa to go to Australia. Now you can get an electronic travel authority in five minutes online, but in the old days it was a bit more complicated. There was generally no problem with the actual granting of the visa, but, as with all things government, problems tended to arise through the act of shuffling the papers.

I was in possession of a passport when I bought my tickets to Australia, the problems arose as a result of my discourse with the travel agent.

"Ahh, it says here there is a visa requirement," the travel agent said as she stared intensely into her computer screen.

"What does that mean?"

"It means you have to send your passport to the Australian consulate along with a form and a check and they send you your passport back with the visa."

"Does it take a long time?"

"Naw … "

"OK, then why don't I go ahead and just buy my ticket now and assume I'll get the visa later?"

Ominous words.

The thing I didn't realize when I began writing a check for the thousand-dollar ticket to Australia is that without the visa in my hand, I had just sentenced myself to three months of desperate waiting and wondering whether or not my passport was going to get to me in time. When you consider that I'm the type of guy who is always going to save fifty dollars by buying a non-refundable ticket … you can see how the stress could magnify.

I filled in the form, signed the check and stuck my passport in an express mailer and shipped it off.

I had elected to use registered mail for the return postage since the travel agent assured me it would only be a matter of weeks. I remember that distinctly because I would play the conversation over and over again in my head as my travel date approached.

"How long will it take?"

"A week at the tops."

"A week?"

"Maybe two … "

A week passed.

Then another.

Then another.

By the fourth I was becoming concerned.

Still no passport in the mail.

Still no visa.

Still no trip.

Eventually, I called the travel agent, and this time as I talked to her, I heard a slight tremor in her voice.

"Ahhh … well, things do get lost in the mail."

"They do, don't they," I replied while experiencing a distinct sinking feeling.

"You know, if you are really nervous about this, you still have enough time to get an expedited passport replacement."

So much for the fifty dollars I'd saved on the non-refundable ticket.

I decided that action was better than all the horrible sitting around and waiting, so I decided to go for the expedited option.

In the far-gone days of more relaxed national security, you could declare your passport lost with relative ease. In a matter of days, my new passport arrived in the mail, and I quickly sent it to the Australian consulate using the post office's fastest shipping service.

A couple days later, my new passport arrived in the mail … on the same day as my old one, both of them with a shiny new visa for Australia glued into one of the inner pages.

My elation at the proper documentation erased my irritation over the excessive cost and run around.

Shortly thereafter I was on the plane, wondering if they were really going to accept the little piece of paper I'd gotten in the mail and let me into their country.

I certainly hoped they would, because I quickly found out that it's no fun doing a twenty-four hour flight the day after a marathon.

There's probably a level of hell that's quite similar to doing two such flights in a row.

CHAPTER 23

There was a period in my life when I was constantly pulled aside and searched at airports. I'm not sure what provoked it since I've been told I have an honest face. My expressions are not necessarily so innocent, but the actual structure of my face could be mistaken for an honest one. Even with that in my favor, airport security never failed to single me out, have me put my hands against the wall and check me for contraband or weapons. This had been going on since I was ten or eleven.

My previous problems with airport security were foremost in my mind as I nervously awaited the arrival of my baggage at the airport in Melbourne. Along with the other travelers, I had shuffled wearily out of the airplane and followed the arrows to the dark and dusty room with the big sign that said "Baggage Claim" hanging dejectedly over the door. The mystical bag gobbler that I had been assured would produce my bag sat before me like an avaricious dragon.

I waited.

And waited.

The machine burped up a bag or two. The passengers around me scurried forth to claim them. Time passed.

After a while the room began to clear out.

After a little while longer, the only fool waiting around was me.

My concern augmented.

It occurred to me how irritating it would be to attempt to ski a cross-country marathon without skis.

The expense of buying a new pair was prohibitive. I was really hoping my skis would turn up.

I waited.

The skis failed to appear.

I decided to wait a little longer.

With a rattle and a shake, the machine's conveyor belt came to a halt. It shuddered once and promptly died with an exhalation of smoke.

Well, I thought, maybe it will start up again.

About then, somebody turned off the lights.

A cleaning crew appeared and began to shine the hard tile floors in the dark.

I was starting to suspect my bag wasn't coming.

I stepped out of the room and looked for someone who was wearing a name tag. I eventually found a guy.

"Hi," I said.

"G'day," he replied. They actually do say that in

Australia, although some of them make an effort not to say it around Americans who tend to squeal in delight when they do. I wasn't squealing in delight at anything just then.

"My bag didn't come out of the baggage claim."

The guy scowled with a "why do you think that's my problem" expression.

We began a conversation that's so redundant and boring that I'm not going to waste your time repeating it. Suffice it to say the fellow asked me about fifty irrelevant questions, and only at the end of all these questions did he finally get around to querying me about the item's description.

"What does the bag look like?"

"It's a blue ski bag."

"Oh … it's oversized?" he said, his eyes widening in fury as if it were my fault this information hadn't been stated previously.

"Yes."

"Then it's right over there."

And he literally pointed like five feet away and there was my bag. I was so excited I didn't even thank the guy—not that he deserved it, necessarily—and I trotted over and retrieved my item.

At that point I was so exhausted, I didn't have the energy to be nervous as I turned over my passport and its potentially suspicious visa that I'd so surreptitiously received in the mail.

Would there be a problem since I'd recently had my passport canceled?

Was a mail-order visa even of any value?

Were they going to deny my entry into the country and make me jump on some super-expensive return flight?

You can probably tell it's a good thing I wasn't born into a time when it would have been necessary to escape from a prison camp or cross checkpoint Charlie with forged documents. I'm ready to turn myself in and confess even when all my documents are in order.

The immigration officer gave my passport a cursory glance, nodded and stamped it.

"Welcome to Australia," he said with a grin. He handed my passport back without any trouble.

I took my passport, smiled, and trotted on out the door.

Through the gate, Kathryn and Ethan were waiting for me.

"Hey! Great to see you! What took so long?"

I decided not to get into the nonsense about my ski bag.

"America is a long ways away!" I replied with a grin.

CHAPTER 24

Australia is not like Wisconsin.

Although it was the middle of winter in Australia, when we walked out of the airport it seemed like a fairly nice early fall day.

In Wisconsin in winter, it gets dark at about three p.m. and there are usually banks of snow piled on the sides of the roads that tower about ten feet high.

"Where's the snow?" I asked.

"It snows in the mountains," Ethan replied, "they get big dumps of like two or three meters of snow and then it slowly melts. Our snow is in a constant state of melting."

"You just hope it dumps enough so you can ski on it for a couple weeks, or at least until the next snowstorm," Kathryn added.

"Hmmmm," I replied.

We piled on into Ethan's Subaru. A Subaru is the auto of choice for skiers all around the world because they get good gas mileage and have all-wheel drive. All-wheel drive is important if you're trying to get your car out of a snowed-in parking lot; two-wheel drive just doesn't cut it.

It felt strange to be thinking of skiing in the middle of July. It felt strange to be experiencing winter in the middle of summer. It felt strange to be in Australia at all, for that matter. You wouldn't think there would be a much different sense of orientation in the Southern Hemisphere, but *you* try go someplace where the sun is in the northern half of the sky, instead of the southern half as it is back home. Unless I really thought about it, I was always finding myself trotting off in the exactly wrong direction. I'd never realized how much of my innate sense of direction was cued in to the relative position of the sun until I went to the land down under.

It was early in the week when I arrived—you can always get cheaper airline tickets when you fly on Tuesdays and Wednesdays—so we puttered around Melbourne for a few days. I had a chance to get used to their money. They use spectacular colors on their bills, unlike the plain old uniform green of the U.S. dollar. The blue for the Australian ten-dollar bill is actually quite stunning.

We did the typical stuff like go to the movies and check out the local shopping centers such as Melbourne Central. Melbourne Central is a notable building in the middle of Melbourne. It is a modern construction that surrounds an old brick building. The brick building is called the Coop's Shot Tower. It was built around 1889 and it's nine stories tall. Years later, I saw Melbourne Central and the Coop's Shot Tower in a Jackie Chan movie called *First Strike*. Interestingly enough, the introductory scenes of that movie were filmed in Fall's Creek where the Kangaroo Hoppet is run—watching that film is a fun way to do reconnaissance for anyone thinking of skiing the Hoppet. We also went to a shopping center that sported two huge statues of Bananas in Pajamas, which was famous because the locals had taken to pulling down the pajamas on a regular basis. It's sort of like the Duke of Wellington statue that always gets the traffic cone put on its head: a minor act of amusing vandalism. You couldn't keep those banana bottoms covered.

One of the fun things about being in another country is listening to the sounds of all the names of the places. In Wisconsin, a lot of our names are based on American Indian words, so we have tourist destinations like Lake Winnebago and the Namekagon River.

However, words of Aboriginal descent were completely different from anything I'd ever heard before. Yet, although they were radically different, they contained an inherent familiarity, as if the sounds that the Aboriginals gravitated to had appeared, either on accident or on purpose, throughout all of human history. For example, you have Geelong, Allanooka, Millaa Millaa, Ginninderra, Mooloolaba, Wagga Wagga, Billabong, etc., not to mention the delightfully named didgeridoo—an instrument that you can always find an Australian willing to play for you. Words of Aboriginal descent are playful and inviting, and I think the sound of them has greatly helped define the nation's culture.

Speaking of Australians, they're absolutely wonderful

people who are always willing to have a good time and are aware that life is short and must be lived to the fullest.

One of the amusing quirks I noticed was the Australian people were extremely sensitive about not being too influenced by American culture. This sensitivity manifested itself in strange ways. For example, rather than watch our terrible daytime TV shows or soap operas, they'd make their own daytime TV shows and soap operas that were modeled almost exactly on the American versions. How this established a unique cultural identity, I don't know. It seems weird that somebody would trash-talk *Friends* and then sit and watch *Neighbors* as if it were infinitely superior.

That being said, I have to say that I am a huge fan of Australian cinema. *Mad Max II* would be an example of a "Hollywoodized" Australian film—it's known as *The Road Warrior* in the U.S.—whereas the original *Mad Max* had a bit more Australian flair, though it's still pretty American. For more Australian-type cinema check out *The Castle* or *The Big Steal*.

The other thing I found was that Australians—at least Kathryn and Ethan—were absolutely crazy about *The Simpsons*. This was back during the Simpsons heyday, so maybe that had something to do with it. However, while I was there, the episode where the Simpsons came to Australia premiered to an extremely lukewarm reception. Neither Kathryn or Ethan could understand why Americans thought Australians punished their criminals by giving them a "booting," as was reported on that particular episode. They looked at me with utter bafflement and the expression on their faces was funnier than anything I'd ever seen on TV.

When we got done with sightseeing and decided to return to ski training, we mostly roller-skied—they gave me a loaner pair—on the bike trails around Melbourne. For those of you who haven't seen it, roller-skiing is a bizarre exercise in which you strap a platform with wheels onto your feet and cross-country ski on asphalt. The platforms are much shorter than regular skis, but they're longer than rollerblades. Actually, there are quite a few skiers who even use rollerblades instead of roller-skis for training because rollerblades don't look nearly as ridiculous. But roller-skis are quite a bit more ski-specific, and the wheels are made to provide a bit more resistance so you have to use your poles as well as your legs to propel yourself. This provides a superior upper-body workout.

Usually we got up in the morning and listened to the weather to see if there had been any snow on Lake Mountain which was the nearest place for cross-country skiing. If there hadn't been any new snow, we hit the roller-skiing trails, but if there had, we made the several-hour trek out to Lake Mountain to enjoy a couple hours on the glorious white stuff. The drive to Lake Mountain culminated in a curvy-uphill road that almost always left my stomach going topsy-turvy by the time we arrived at the ski center. Along the way, I was usually on the lookout for wombats—solid, stocky Australian marsupials—and we saw a couple before my trip was over.

It doesn't matter where you go in the world, ski centers are always built with a rather Nordic-looking design. However, the fun part is observing how the Nordic influence has been softened to fit into the local surroundings. For example, in Wisconsin the Nordic-inspired buildings sit amongst oak, pine and popple trees. In Australia they are almost universally surrounded by gum trees, a much different-looking tree. Still, the Nordic center's distinctive steep roofs and curled, dragon-like ornamentation, made me feel at home even if the backdrop was not familiar.

Lake Mountain is a beautiful ski center with a lovely view and a glorious selection of well maintained trails. It reminded me of many of the ski centers of small towns across Wisconsin. Every now and then as you get on the race circuit back in the Midwest, you stumble across some oasis that is clearly the work of an industrious fellow who has fully dedicated himself to the maintenance of a lovely ski trail. Lake Mountain gave me that impression.

The strange thing about Lake Mountain was that sometimes we seemed to be skiing over the tops of trees that had been almost completely buried by snow. Other days, three, four, or five feet of snow would have melted and we would be skiing down by the bases. It was as Kathryn and Ethan had stated, the snow was constantly melting and running off. This meant we could always use high-fluoro waxes and depend on above freezing temperatures, but it also meant the track was often soft like mashed potatoes and the exercise was difficult.

We spent a month or so training at Lake Mountain and at Falls Creek when we could get there. I had arrived in Australia fit, but I had to convert my marathon fitness into cross-country-ski fitness.

The Kangaroo Hoppet is usually run at the end of August, so I had little time. As always, the days flew by in a blur.

CHAPTER 25

A week before the great Australian race, right when the excitement was starting to build, I got the flu. Ethan had been pretty sure I was over-training, and he'd been telling me so for a long time, but I was too stubborn to admit it. One of my flaws is an overdeveloped sense of competition. I try to disguise it in all manner of ways, but it occasionally foils me.

Nights were tough. I'd stay up all night vomiting and then sit around all day trying to keep soda crackers and Sprite in my stomach.

Needless to say, there was no skiing.

For the last week of training tune-up, I sat inside while everyone else did their final preparations. They'd go out in the morning, atwitter with the joy of youth and health, and I'd wallow in my blanket and wish I were dead.

The days evaporated from the calendar as the Hoppet ominously approached.

Every morning I woke up with the hope that I had started to feel better.

Every morning I was sorely disappointed.

But there was no way I was going to fly all that way and not do the race.

Who could tell if I'd ever even get back to Australia again in my lifetime?

No, I had to do the Kangaroo Hoppet, no matter how I felt.

The day before the race, I headed to the race office in my bathrobe with a bowl of soup under my arm and an ice pack on my head.

"Can I help you, sir?" the attendant said.

"Yeah, I'm here to pick up my bib with my race number."

"You … "

"Yeah, me! Gotta problem with that?"

"Not at all."

Bib under arm, I stumbled back to the hotel.

Everybody was engaging in the typical pre-race festivities, discussing strategy, putting on wax, eying each other up and wondering who would be the fastest. I walked into the room and all of a sudden it was like somebody had invited the grim reaper to dinner.

"Uhhh … " a lone voice said, "are you sure you are going to race tomorrow?"

"Hell yes, I'm racing … I didn't come all this way to be sick."

"But you *are* sick."

"It's all in the mind … I'm doing it!"

In my delirium, I tried to melt a banana into the bases of my skis with a steaming iron. Somebody took the appliance from my hands and put me to bed, but only after promising they'd prepare my skis for me.

"Yes, we promise, we'll let you race … but you need to rest now!"

***

Race morning is always the same. The whole goal is to get up at the crack of nothing and try to scarf down bland food that will stay put in a nervous, somersaulting belly.

I wasn't even going to try to eat. I hadn't eaten anything in four days—eating something then would have been a total disaster.

I put on my ski clothes.

For the first time, I was set to do a race in Lycra tights rather than wind pants. The reason was the heat. The forecast for the mountain at Falls Creek was well into the forties. Actually, it's typical of the Hoppet that the race date is either changed or canceled because it gets too warm and the snow melts. It all depends on whether they have a big dump of snow close to race day.

That year, they hadn't.

Ethan was already saying how we'd be doing two loops up in the mountains instead of having our second loop go around the lake.

"What's that going to do to the course's difficulty?" I asked.

He scowled and jammed his thumb up into the air several times.

I got the message.

I wasn't getting any breaks.

At least it was going to be warm enough that I probably wouldn't freeze to death.

I got on my ski clothes and headed out with the rest of them. The Hoppet office had done me the courtesy of giving me number 18. Low numbers were for the front row and we all assumed they had given me that start number based on the fact that I was a young guy who had come all the way from America. It had been a nice gesture on their part, but I wasn't thrilled about the extra attention.

We lined up on a small rise overlooking the dam wall. The ski area at Falls Creek looks like a military complex. It's a beautiful area, don't get me wrong, but there is a stone dam with a huge reservoir that the ski trails cross over and go around.

I stood slightly toward the back.

"Hey 18," somebody said, "you're supposed to be up front."

I couldn't even muster the strength to respond.

The starting gun went off with a crack.

I stumbled along, foot after foot vaguely ever forward. In my delirium, it seemed like there were legs and poles and neon covered skis everywhere. I was caught in the middle of it like a lost vagabond in a day-glo hurricane.

For about a hundred yards, I thought I might be OK.

Then my sickness and my weakness kicked in and I realized I was in for a hellish day.

The Kangaroo Hoppet is not like the Birkie. The Birkie is filled with short, steep hills that come at you one after another as you pass through a glorious pine forest.

The Hoppet, on the other hand, is filled with agonizingly long, gradual hills that wind around and through spectacular mountain country.

The Birkie is like getting hit with one hundred sharp, angry jabs.

The Hoppet is like getting destroyed by ten roundhouse punches.

After either, you've taken a beating.

I toddled along, feeling fairly humiliated that I felt so ill and unable to give a good accounting of myself. People passed me. People who had no business passing me. I was disgusted and miserable.

The worst of it was that nobody out there even had a clue as to what kind of effort I was giving.

I should have stayed in bed.

Everybody had encouraged me to stay in bed.

They seemed to think it was foolish, rather than valiant, to attempt the event, and maybe they were right.

I trundled along, sometimes sweating more from my

fever than my exertion. I was thankful the race was in Australia, so it wasn't sub-freezing and I could stop and collect myself occasionally. The uphills, I walked. The downhills, I glided. The crowds passed me and disappeared. Then they came around for their second lap, passed me again, and disappeared.

I was all by myself.

The clock ticked away and there was nothing I could do about it.

There's never anything that you can do about the passage of time.

It was pure agony.

And finally, when I didn't think I'd ever be free of the torment, the finish line reared its ugly head.

I slumped over and slid toward it.

The announcer called my name.

I sat in a snow bank for a long while before finally getting up to change my clothes and head back to bed.

At the end of the day, the only thing that matters is your time.

I'd just done a forty-two kilometer race in close to six hours.

There was no asterisk next to the printed result in the paper to say that I'd been ill.

Just the time that had been recorded. The next day I got my Worldloppet passport stamped and I headed home shortly after that.

On the plane, I fingered my Worldloppet passport and regarded the number that was printed there for the Kangaroo Hoppet.

Six hours was too long under any circumstances.

I resolved not to let that happen again.

Sometimes taking a beating like that can be a good thing.

CHAPTER 26

When I got back to the U.S., it was fall, so it was full-on roller-skiing season and I was inspired. I'd enrolled in the University of Wisconsin-Eau Claire, so I had classes to keep me busy, but in my free time I pestered Dean a lot on the phone.

"Hey Dean … got any roller-skis yet?"

"I told you … NO!"

"Well, get some!"

Click.

Fresh off my disaster in Australia, I was ready to buckle down and get fit. However, like an idiot, I'd bought some V2 roller-skis with medium-speed wheels. I was under the impression that medium-speed wheels would give me a better workout. I didn't realize how tedious it would be to actually ski on them. In the last few years, V2 has unveiled some really good products, but in the mid-'90s, they still had some kinks to work out. I guess I was stuck with V2s because they were the popular roller-ski at the time—or perhaps it was because they were the only roller-ski I could find.

To purchase a set of roller-skis is to be on the fringes of consumer civilization. They aren't the type of things that normal people could even venture a guess as to where they could be found. In truth, to get them, you have to go on a yearlong mythical quest—or three years, in my case. You have to work yourself up to that distant mental place where it seems like buying such a ridiculous niche item makes sense. Roller-skis are the type of product that you obtain by filling out a poorly photocopied flier on the back of a piece of corrugated cardboard, which itself came from some other item that was nearly impossible to get your hands on. In short, you don't just go down to stores to buy roller-skis, not even ski stores. You have to prove yourself worthy of the roller-ski.

Like I said, I'd gotten some V2 skis with medium wheels. I'd gotten the medium wheels in part because of their superior workout potential, and in part because roller-skis don't have breaks.

Generally, you don't get going all that fast on roller-skis, but when you crash it's all asphalt and gravel waiting below to snap and gnaw at your exposed and tender flesh. Roller-skiing is inherently a bit more unstable than rollerblading, or even snow skiing. To begin with, roller-skis are heavy. There's no need to make them light because nobody races on roller-skis—well, a few people do, but they're hardly commercial races. Also, the finicky construction of roller-ski wheels require an absolutely clean roadway—any small rocks on the pavement will get jammed in the axle, causing you to go bum over cranium, if you're lucky.

You wouldn't think by looking at them that most roads are covered with tiny axle-biting pebbles.

Well … try going for a roller-ski sometime. I guarantee you'll find the rocks.

I kept pestering Dean and pestering Dean and pestering Dean until finally he acquired a pair of roller-skis. He actually acquired two pairs, *neither* of them V2s. This utterly blew my mind considering the amount of time I'd spent looking for roller-skis coupled with the fact that I hadn't even found any traces of anything other than V2s. To have him show up with not one but *two* alternate brands was mind-boggling.

Well, if you ever get to know Dean, you'll soon discover that he's got his sources.

It was only later that I discovered the last weird and amazing thing about roller-skis—despite the fact that they are so hard to find, everybody who has roller-skis seems to have a different *kind* of roller-skis. And these aren't homemade pieces of aluminum that people have hammered together in their garages, although you'll see those out there, too. These are commercial products with their own logos and everything. One might wonder where these items come from. Who is out there making them? What do they do in their spare time besides trying to conceive of ways to improve the rare and beautiful roller-ski?

Anyway, Dean had a couple of pairs of roller-skis and we decided to meet at Shell Lake, where they had recently put down a new layer of asphalt. I sat in the shade and again experienced that odd sensation of putting on my ski boots in the middle of summer. It's a good feeling, it's like you're getting the jump on everyone else. I remembered my first Birkie and how I had wondered at the end how the elite racers had gotten their speed.

This was how.

Or at least part of it.

They found their speed by skiing on metallic death traps in the middle of a hot summer day.

Dean rolled up in his car next to where I was parked and I jumped out to go and greet him..

"Check these out!" he said smiling. He pulled out an angular piece of metal that looked like an elongated wedge.

"What's that for, splitting wood?"

"No, it's a roller-ski!"

My head tilted like a confused dog. It was only after the declaration that I noticed that the odd item had a wheel on either end.

I squinted.

"Wait … even the wheels are angled!"

It was true, they weren't circles so much as cones. It seemed to defy the laws of physics. How was that supposed to work?

"You're going to get yourself killed on those," I said.

"No, I have it on good authority that these are awesome! I'm psyched to try them!"

I nodded and went back to my car to get out the rest of my equipment.

Don't kid yourself, there is a lot of equipment involved even with something as basic as cross-country skiing. A short list of essential items includes the following items:

Lightweight gloves: Otherwise you rip up your hands on your poles.

Poles: Some people free-skate on roller-skis, but poles are important for an upper-body workout.

Special carbide tips for your poles: Because the tips on regular ski poles tend to break on asphalt.

A diamond sharpener for your carbide tips: Because the tips don't give you leverage if they go skipping out from under you due to being horrifically dull.

Pole straps: These are attached to the poles, but you've got to wiggle your hands into them, which is a bit of an annoyance. Make sure this is the last thing you do before you go roller-skiing because it's close to impossible to handle your car keys with your poles strapped on.

Water bottle holder with gear pouch: You need to drink while you're out there, and the pouch is for holding your energy bar and aforementioned car keys.

Sunglasses: Something awesome preferably … you already look goofy enough because you're roller-skiing.

Athletic hat: A baseball cap won't do because those are too thick and they get all sweaty. You need something that you can put on backwards to increase the cool effect.

Ski boots: They are expensive and roller-skiing kind of beats the heck out of them. You should probably invest in an inexpensive pair of boots for roller-skiing and use them instead of the racing-model ski boot you use for the Birkie.

The roller-skis themselves: Not easy to acquire.

Helmet: To protect your noggin.

With my equipment checklist properly accounted for, I stood in the shade getting myself together and thinking that I needed a squire like a noble knight of old just to get all my gear properly strapped on. After about forty-five minutes, I was ready to go. I glanced at Dean. My head tilted sideways again.

His unusual roller-skis seemed even stranger now that he was attempting to balance on them. He looked like he was standing on the jaws of a crocodile as each ski was tilted toward the central pivot point that he occupied.

"Dean … seriously, you're going to get yourself killed on those things."

"Naw … these are awesome, they're racing roller-skis."

"OK."

We headed out.

I'd been out in Australia on roller-skis but I was still a novice. That being the case, it took me all of two seconds to wish I'd bought the "fast" wheels instead of the "medium" ones.

The slow wheels felt like I was swimming through concrete.

It felt like I was sawing wood with every stride.

"Gnnnnaaaa … .this is slooooow!"

I looked back at Dean.

Dean's roller-ski wheels seemed to be made of plastic. They bounced and echoed like someone beating a milk-jug kettle drum.

"How's it going?"

"These … things … are … awesome … " Dean said through gritted teeth, his brow furrowed in frantic concentration.

We pretended we were on top of things and that everything was cool as we trundled along.

I'm glad there's no video of our first few hundred meters. It certainly would have gone viral and we would have been unemployable for the rest of our lives based on the fact that we were uncoordinated fools.

But things got easier. I figured out that if you went a bit faster, the V2 wheels, as resistant as they were to rolling, tended to warm up and spin as if only a vast majority of their essence as physical items was opposed to that task—instead of the entirety of it.

We chatted away.

The heat from the newly paved lake road rose up to meet us in friendly, oscillating waves.

The leaves changed from summer green to autumn yellow right before our eyes.

We had one brilliant idea after another.

"Let's race to that sign!" I cried suddenly, and started sprinting like a mad man.

In my twenties, all I ever wanted to do was race.

Dean was never one to back down from a challenge, and as soon as I started to exert myself, I heard him behind me thumping and heaving like an elephant in a packaging crate.

The sound of his plastic roller-ski wheels combined with the tic … tic … tic of his poles jamming into the blacktop to create a wall of bizarre, artificial sound.

We accelerated to five miles per hour.

The wind almost began to be noticeable across our perspiring foreheads.

We dove into the task!

Suddenly, there was an explosion of noise like a car accident. I looked back, careful not to lose my own balance, and saw Dean crumpled in a pile of roller-skis, poles, and limbs. There were at least five limbs too many. Was he dead? Had he bashed his head on the asphalt and lost his senses forever?

I decided to act quickly and after crossing the designated finish line and therefore winning the sprint—first things first, after all—I spun around and headed back.

"Dean! Are you OK?"

"Yeah … I just caught a rock," he grumbled.

"Are you OK?"

"Yeah, I'm fine."

What a relief, I wouldn't have to spend the rest of my life feeding him pea slop through a straw. Still, the guy had given me a fright … something needed to be said.

"Those skis … "

"They're awesome," Dean replied flatly. He delicately touched a couple bloody patches on his legs and then did his best to simply ignore them.

I decided not to push it.

We continued along the lake and our brief moment of fear quickly evaporated. In fact, it was erased to the point where Dean actually seemed to start noticeably relaxing on his skis.

"I think I've figured out the trick to these skis," he said with a smile. "They are really fast."

I looked up and noticed another sign in the distance.

"Race to that sign?" I said.

Dean didn't need to be asked twice.

Again, we invoked the sound of heavy machinery in a wrestling match to the death as our poles and skis and wheels echoed with the distinctive frequency of whatever unique vibrating polymer or alkaloid had gone into their composition.

I accelerated but Dean was right there. He was just on the verge of pulling ahead, when there was another explosion of plastic and exclamations as Dean went windmilling out of sight and into the ditch.

Finishing the sprint, I spun around nervously and went back to see if Dean had survived.

"What … " I started, but Dean interrupted me.

"They're awesome … they're awesome … " he groaned as he extracted himself from a culvert and the snapping turtle family that had taken up residence there.

"What … "

"Just hit a twig … I've got it for the next time."

As much as I liked winning these sprints, it was starting to seem a little too sadistic even for me.

"Maybe we should just cool it and finish out our hour by taking it easy."

"No man … one more … one more … "

"OK," I said reluctantly, "but let's go easy for a little while first."

Dean reluctantly agreed.

Again the storm clouds evaporated.

Again it was a nice late summer, early fall day.

The trees waved at us kindly in the crisp breeze.

The animals came out to frolic in the sun.

"There's a sign!" Dean screamed, and he was off. He looked like a giraffe on roller skates, and considering how agile and athletic a guy Dean is, the sight was a testament to how poorly designed those roller-skis of his actually were.

For a moment, it looked like he might make it.

But then, like a guy trying to walk a tightrope while juggling and wearing swimming flippers, it all came apart.

The last crash was the most spectacular of all.

Rocks flew into the air.

There was the sound of carbon fiber crackling in the wind.

Dean did seven cartwheels and drove into the soft topsoil like the meteor that brought Superman to Earth.

He lay there immobile among the wreckage, tendrils of steam curling up into the air.

After a leisurely ski across the designated sprint finish line, I went back to check on him.

"Dean," I cried, "Dean … wake up!"

"W-wha?"

"Dean!"

"Awesome ... awesome ... just gotta get the hang of them ..."

"Dean?" at this, Dean's eyes seemed to finally focus on me, "Who gave you those roller-skis anyway?" I asked earnestly.

"You know," Dean said reflectively, "I'd never seen him before. I met him out at the crossroads. He was wearing a red suit with a whipped tail and was carrying a pitchfork."

"Did he make you sign for them?" I asked.

"Naw," Dean said, shaking his head.

"A little tip," I replied, "If you see him in the future, don't stop for a chat."

After a few minutes of exertion, Dean extracted himself from the hole he had dug out of the ground. We skied back to the car without incident.

The next time I saw him, he had a different pair of roller-skis.

I never saw the "racing roller-skis" again, and Dean declined to inform me what had become of them. I think foul play might have been involved.

CHAPTER 27

Somehow we survived roller-ski season and for the first time, Dean and I approached winter feeling like we were truly prepared. The Australian contingent made its appearance and some lunatic got the brilliant idea that we should do every single weekend marathon of significance in Wisconsin, Michigan and Minnesota, perhaps with a trip to Canada thrown in for good measure.

It was insanity, there had to be at least twelve marathons during the season.

Of course, we unanimously agreed to do it.

It became sort of an endless winter road trip (with apologies to Luke Bodensteiner). The logistics of getting to these events was an eternal nightmare. Not only did we have to locate places with names like Biwabik, Mora, Ironwood and Calumet on the map, we had to drive there, find a place to sleep, and be rested and ready come race day.

There was even one weekend when we did the twenty-six-kilometer Pre-Birkie on Saturday, and followed it with the fifty-eight-kilometer Mora Vasaloppet on Sunday. We thought we were tough after that until we found out that the guy who won the Vasaloppet had not only done a ski race the day before, but had finished second place in a forty-two-kilometer event.

We discovered that when you're following around the ski season like it's a touring Irish band, you start to notice that snow actually takes quite a bit of abuse. As you blow into town after town, you become accustomed to seeing slushy mounds of ice and powder in all its vibrant and horrible forms. Sometimes there's this terrible wet gray snow that accumulates beneath your tire wells that you have to kick out when you go to fill up for gas. Then there's the snow on the side of the road that gets pushed aside by snowplows and is left to harden into strange and unnatural formations. There's also falling snow that you encounter while driving that can either land on your windshield in delicate flakes, or crash into it in exploding spatters.

Being a skiing nomad is like living inside snow.

It's like you've been absorbed by a vast snow amoeba.

And the only time that snow seems pure and pristine and unspoiled is when you get out on a freshly groomed ski course and do your race.

It was during this long and bizarre winter that I realized how much skiing had taken hold.

Skiing now determined what I ate.

Skiing determined how much I slept.

Skiing determined what I did on the weekends.

Skiing determined the people I hung out with.

And I didn't regret a minute of it because they were all good people, honest people, healthy people who were pursuing something admittedly ridiculous—I mean, seriously, who spends all their free time running around in the freezing cold with boards on their feet and virtually no clothing on their bodies— but euphoria-inducing.

We were insane!

We were addicted to abusing ourselves in cold and distant places!

So recently the idea of being seen in public in a Lycra suit had seemed terrifying, like the type of nightmares you used to have back in high school, but now I didn't have the slightest qualms about marching into an Old Country Buffet in my ski gear after a three-hour training session. We'd pull up to the buffet and load our plates to the chuckles of the good old boys in the place who thought they knew how to eat, and we'd quickly have them choking on their derision as we polished off plate after plate beyond the most they'd ever seen consumed in one sitting in their wildest dreams.

We were burning calories!

The furnace was HOT!

We had to keep it STOKED!

The best part of training and skiing like a madman is that you literally can't eat enough. You're always short on calories, so you always have to keep packing it in. It's glorious!

Some hotels in the far-off corners of the frozen plains

have waffle irons and batter for making breakfast. When we got done with those places, it was like a tornado had come through—there was batter, syrup and butter dripping from the ceiling!

As we continued to travel and race, a strange thing happened.

We started to recognize faces at the various events of the area.

The distinctive ski suit of a competitor appeared again and again at multiple events.

Little by little, we came to understand.

There was a whole nomadic community of mad amateur skiers who traipsed around from event to event just like we did. I've since learned that, if you look, you'll find interesting, wonderful, counter-culture communities like this springing up or continuing a local tradition everywhere you go.

As the year went on, we got to know them more. They taught us the tricks, like where the most economical hotels were in Wausau, or where the secret bathrooms were hidden at various ski venues. There is always a line for the bathroom at a ski race, and there is always a secret bathroom to be found if you know where to look.

We took down names.

We got e-mail addresses.

And, all too soon, the winter evaporated like a dream.

The Birkie came, the third for me and the first for Dean. After all the training we'd been doing, we had wonderfully fast races, and we both qualified for the first wave the following year.

It felt as if we had arrived as skiers.

We had found the community.

The only thing left to do was to bring it even closer together.

CHAPTER 28

Now that we thought of ourselves as "real" skiers, Dean and I decided we were fed up by the fact that all the ski suits for sale in the local bike and ski shops were horrifically ugly. Additionally, we had gotten sick of doing free advertising on behalf of whoever made those suits and had plastered their logos all over every inch of our bodies.

If we were going to advertise something, we decided it should be something that we had some stock in.

That thought in mind, we marched into a new bike/ ski shop in Twin Pines called The Kick and Glide and demanded that they sponsor us.

Amazingly, despite the fact that they probably had every reason to throw us out of the shop for being arrogant goofballs, they agreed. The truth is that being a first-wave Birkie skier carries a significant amount of clout in Northern Wisconsin, especially among people who own ski shops.

The concept of the local amateur bike team had been around for quite a while. Dean had been riding with Mel Wallace and his crew down in Osceola for the last couple of summers. The idea of a local team is that you get a large enough group of people together to justify a custom order of jerseys, shorts, and whatnot; pound the pavement in search of a couple sponsors whose logos you display proudly on your jersey; design some cool-looking bike wear—always a trick—and then proudly race and train together, recruiting more members with every ride. Having a team is a great way to meet people, and it allows you to make a couple mass orders on common items that you need to replenish every year, like ski wax or bicycle tubes.

Dean and I got to work and we hacked out a deal with Kick and Glide. No money was involved, we just needed to be affiliated with a store. We then designed the most awesome ski suit in the history of ski suits, got thirty people to pre-order them, and presto, the Kick and Glide Nordic Ski Team was born

In case you didn't know, being on a team changes you profoundly.

It's amazing how much differently I found myself approaching my training, my races, and my personal fitness when I was part of a team. Before the team, I was just a free agent, a mercenary.

But with the team I had colors to represent..

There's a reason ancient forces used to carry a banner into battle. Just the sight of team colors makes your blood rush with a sensation of belonging.

Dean and I were already motivated to get fit and ski well, but starting up the team gave us a whole new resource for training motivation. Now I couldn't just roll over and hit snooze on the morning of a training race after a hard week of work. People were expecting me to be there and I felt I couldn't let them down. I had also gained a vast pool of friends who called me up and invited me to go for training runs or bike rides with them on days I might have otherwise been tempted to sit at home and watch TV.

To adapt a familiar phrase, it takes a village to ski the Birkie.

At that time, nothing like our club really existed in the Northwoods, which is odd since there's so much potential for socializing among the skiing community. The simple fact is that if you've skied a marathon in negative-forty-degree temperatures with someone, you know that person on a level that can't be matched. Heck, you could have lived with that person for forty years and not had the insight that you achieved after one three-hour race.

Your skier friends have got your back.

Mel Wallace was especially excited about the team. He'd had a couple of top-fifty finishes at the Birkie and he was always on the lookout for new training partners to help him in his quest to "shock the world."

"I'm taking the Birkie down!" he sometimes cried while training. I always imagine him with his face painted half blue and half white, clutching the mane of a charging stallion that's hurtling through a ball of fire. Mel was good at motivational speaking, which is important after a four hour roller-ski session that utterly beats you down.

He had the kind of enthusiasm we needed.

Along with other Kick and Glide members, Dean, Mel and I traded training tips, got on each other's cases, raced each other madly when there were no "official" races to be found, and kept the Birkie circled on our calendars throughout the year.

Before it was all said and done, Mel actually did come pretty close to shocking the world.

But by then he wasn't able to shock us.

Team racing and training had made us believe in him, in ourselves, and in the whole skiing community.

Birkie fever is special; sometimes it blossoms into a full-fledged case of Birkie-itis!

We had all become certifiable cases.

CHAPTER 29

I started doing the newsletters for our team, a job that I performed with a terrible seriousness. I limited myself to a single page, ripe with allegory and alliteration in order to keep the iron hot and the morale high. At first, it was a little intimidating sending out a rallying call once a month to every skier I knew. You have to be careful when you write anything to a mass audience because you never know what people will be offended by—how was I supposed to know that guy had family in Lithuania?

But after a few shaky tries, I got the hang of it and soon, based mainly on the sheer literary brilliance of my newsletters—they were often compared to Checkov; not the guy from "Star Trek," but Anton Checkov—our numbers swelled beyond anything we could have hoped for. I was also always sure to end each letter with either a fun fact or a haiku.

Here's a sample:

THE NORDIC DOMINATOR
The official publication of the
Kick and Glide Nordic Ski Team

Good news from the Gods! We can call off the human sacrifice, it seems our utter domination has provided adequate pagan appeasement. The recent string of Kick and Glide triumphs has triggered the celestial joy button. Normally I don't like to sit here and spend too much time on individual recognition. For one thing that would take up the whole newsletter. In case you haven't noticed our team is a powerhouse. Even if I tried to give proper notice to every one of our members' accomplishments I would inevitably leave somebody out. Furthermore, I figure people are more interested in hearing about the Gods and their latest futile attempts to place obstacles in our path.

The Birkie is coming, although it might include a swim this year if the weather stays like it is (maybe we should go through with the human sacrifice after all). Truth be told I've been a little bit nervous about that for the last few months. The sacrificial dagger isn't as sharp as it could be and I'm a little hesitant to try sharpening it on the stone grinder like the Dominator suggested. Besides, I'm thinking that whole swarm of locusts nonsense was just a bluff.

But time and space is growing short, I think I'd like to leave you now with a selection from a touching novel I cherish deeply, The Lotus Blossom by Henrich Gottlieb: "The next morning I was shocked to discover that not only was I naked and covered in blood, I had no recollection of where I was or how I had come to be there … .(157)" (sigh) That always brings a tear to my eye, it captures the essence of the human conflict so succinctly.

Ski prep tip: Soft flex, lots of structure, and really, really, really expensive wax. If that doesn't provide enough speed then just work yourself so hard that you vomit, if nothing else it makes for a great story afterwards! VIVA LA RESISTANCE! (insert French accent here)

Fun fact #6: There is absolutely no occasion for which a human head is an appropriate gift.

***

If I remember right, the Birkie was shortened that year due to a lack of snow. This is the terrible risk you take when you put all of your emotional momentum for a year on a ski race which is based on conditions beyond human control. However, despite the uncertainty of the weather, the heroic race almost always finds a way to manifest itself.

Remember the Birkie is run in Wisconsin.

Betting on there being snow in Wisconsin in winter is as close to a sure thing as you can find in an event where there are no referees to bribe.

If they shorten the race, or they change the date, you adapt and move on and enjoy the ride.

Above all, cross-country skiing teaches you to roll with the punches and if your buddies are right there rolling alongside you, then you've got a party on your hands no matter what the circumstances.

The training and the racing and living must go on, on, ever on!

CHAPTER 30

When you're doing a lot of training and racing, sooner or later you're going to be hit by something known as "the Bonk." For those of you who don't know what I'm talking about, it's surely the terminology and not the sensation that you don't recognize. Anybody who has ever religiously saddled up on his dime-wide, sew-up rims or pulled tight the laces of a sleek Asics running shoe or clipped on a pair of cross-country skis has, at one time or another, experienced the Bonk.

The Bonk is the sensation you get during intense exercise in which your blood sugar drops and your body simply stops working. It's not especially dangerous and it's easy enough to prevent, but it can cause an extreme amount of discomfort and weakness. Generally, all you have to do when you feel the Bonk coming on is chow down on a candy bar or some other food item and like magic you'll be good to go once again. But in that initial moment of Bonking, you become seriously lethargic.

The Bonk is different than muscle exhaustion because you simply can't push yourself through it. Trying to overcome the Bonk mentally is sort of like trying to will yourself sober. When something is caused by a chemical change in your bloodstream, you really can't ignore it or make it go away.

You need food! You need calories! You need sugar!

Athletes in the throes of the Bonk have been known to eat things that would make a billy goat go pale.

The Bonk creeps up on you like a leopard and then pounces like a gorilla. From the moment it hits you, you're as weak as a kitten and twice as disoriented.

Now, you'd think, being the mature, experienced endurance athletes that I and the other members of Kick and Glide were, the Bonk would be easy to avoid. But on more than one occasion, Dean, Mel and I got ourselves torched by the Bonk monster in the middle of some ridiculous endurance workout.

To ensure your avoidance of the Bonk, all you need to do is pack enough emergency food or money. You can't eat the money obviously, but you can use it to buy those cheap gas-station sandwiches that have been sitting on the shelves since 1950.

Even the best preparation is not foolproof, however, and you can be sure that one day the Bonk is going to creep up on you. The fact is that if you're trying to do five hundred training hours a year in between the obligations of work, family, and whatever else you might do to occupy your time—I'm sure it's innocent, I'm not insinuating anything—inevitably there will come a day when you find yourself in the middle of nowhere with a growling stomach and not so much as an acorn to appease it.

That's when things get ugly, and you find out the truth about yourself. Truth that you may have been happier not knowing.

The Bonk, my friends, is a long way from adolescent grumpiness due to having the munchies. The Bonk is a feral response to a threat against your very survival. In the throes of a Bonk binge there is very little you will not consume. The body is dying, it needs sustenance, you will obey this primordial call.

Dean was usually the culprit who got me into trouble. As the years went by, he had become truly elite in just about every sport he practiced.

"Hey man," he said one day in the midst of what I had begun to think of as his one-hundred-year program of rigorous ultra-human training, "let's go for a bike ride."

"Er … well," I responded, trying desperately to think up a way to escape this terrifying prospect while preserving my manhood, "I haven't been riding much lately, I wouldn't want to slow you down."

"Nonsense, we'll go slow, it'll be fun! Three hours, tops."

Curses, the man was persuasive.

"Only three hours?"

"Yeah, just a nice little spin."

"Well, OK."

Three hours and ninety-seven miles later I found myself gasping in a ditch near some town called Earl, Wisconsin, trying to wrestle some honey away from a horde of swarming bees and the massive grizzly bear that had been tending them. Of course, I hadn't brought any food or money. Money would have been worthless anyway since there wasn't a store or another human being for two hundred miles in any direction. Meanwhile, Dean, oblivious to my plight, stood by the road and scratched his head.

"Oops, I guess we should have taken a left back at Highway AA."

There was a whole alphabet of highways between me and salvation. It was like being trapped in the level of hell reserved for evil librarians.

The Bonk!

Ask anyone who you see regularly in athletic tights and they'll have a story to tell you. In moments of the Bonk, it's surprising the things that you'll eat. "Fear Factor" has nothing on a starving athlete.

I've climbed over fences to steal apples from orchards. I've scraped the mold off a piece of stale bread that had lodged itself between my car seat cushions into a place only a starving man would think to look for food. I've dug out promotional packets of fluorescent power gel that had been abandoned in my water bottle pack for untold years.

"What the hell is this stuff?" I demanded on one such

occasion. Dean and I were standing on the Birkie trail about ten kilometers north of OO.

"I had a packet of that once," Dean replied, semi-deliriously, he was Bonking too, but I was too Bonked to notice. "I think they had to stop selling it because it killed somebody or gave somebody cancer or something."

"I don't care," I snapped, ripping open the top and gobbling down the horrific stuff in one vicious motion.

The beast was momentarily appeased. We limped back to our car and found some gas station donuts to bring us back from the brink of flesh eating zombie land.

But the worst Bonk moment for me came during Grandma's Marathon. This was probably about 1999, it was a hot year and kind of a strange day. People were passing out left and right. I wasn't in exceptionally good shape that year, but that didn't stop me from running along with this spectacularly beautiful blonde girl who was an absolute joy to talk with. She was on pace for a 3:40 marathon or so, a respectable time. That wasn't a mark I was going to hit that day, but there are some callings that are higher and more powerful than common sense.

Come to think of it, I can't remember the last time my common sense called in anything louder than a dull whisper.

"So, how about if we slow down a bit and enjoy this marathon?" I said, knowing that if we didn't slow down soon I was going to die.

"Come on, run with me, you can do it!"

What an angel. Testosterone let me fake it for ten miles, then the wheels fell off and burned.

"I've got to slow down," I said and veered away. She went prancing off into the crowd never to be seen again.

I faked it for about five more miles before it hit me. The slight tremble in my hands, the blurred vision, the cold sweat, the agony, the weakness. Oh no! It was the Bonk!

I patted myself for food; I found none. In the past I'd been smart enough to staple a couple GU energy gel packets to my clothing, but not on that day. Curses! I lumbered awkwardly on, already realizing that my mental agility was beginning to slow.

What was I going to do?

An aid station! This was one of the area's biggest competitions, they had to have food somewhere!

The next aid station appeared on the horizon and my heart soared. This was it, I had made it! They had to have food! I gazed with weary eyes in intense, focused, concentration at all the little hands that held forth Dixie cups filled with water or soaked sponges. Water wasn't going to help me. I scoured the offerings.

Water.

Water.

Water.

The first ten hands did not scare me. I was confident the food would be coming later.

Water.

Water.

Water.

I began to grow nervous. They had to have food, didn't they? Don't tell me they didn't have anything to eat at the aid station.

Water.

Sponge.

Wait, what's that? Some yellowish goo, is it … Drat, it's a platter of Vaseline.

Water.

I had run almost completely through the aid station with no sight of anything to eat. All hope fluttered from my battered body and I had just begun to succumb to despair when I saw it! There, at the end, was an angelic hand holding a single Twizzler. I put on the brakes and snatched the meager offering like some wild creature pouncing upon an unsuspecting forest rodent. No Twizzler was ever eaten so fast. I pushed myself on, trying desperately to will the sugar into my addled bloodstream.

Strength momentarily returned. But it was all too soon that I discovered how much energy a Twizzler contains. Almost nothing.

My reprieve had been temporary. I needed something else.

The next aid station was miles away. Despair began to creep in once again. I wasn't going to be able to make it. I was starving. In my mind's eye, I imagined my body turning against itself, the internal corpuscles harvesting bits of redundant flesh to toss into the raging furnace.

The situation was dire. I stared at the black road that stretched out before me. The other runners flashed in and out of focus. The blurry asphalt resembled a celestial night with little shiny patches glowing in the darkness. What were those patches?

I squinted.

They were racer's gel packets! GU packets! Empty GU packets that had been cast aside as if to torment me. Everybody else had brought food, why hadn't I? What had I been thinking?

I continued running. The yards dragged past.

The GU packets continued to torment me. They had so recently been full with the nourishing calories I so desperately needed. What a cruel trick to play. To be so close and yet so far from my salvation! If only they were full, if only some GU still remained …

A nasty thought occurred to me.

I discarded it. It was too horrible to contemplate.

Three more agonizing yards passed. My body was at the brink, I needed to eat.

The distasteful idea returned.

Perhaps … perhaps some of those GU packets still had a bit of GU in them?

No! I put the thought out of my mind the way that crash survivors probably do when they first consider cannibalizing the other crash victims. But we all know how conflicts like that turn out.

No! I screamed internally realizing that some deep, inner part of my mind was trying to convince me to take the path of madness. Harvesting nasty discarded GU packets from the street is too terrible! What if I get some kind of disease from the leftover saliva?

Actually, that's absurd, these are marathoners. They're all doctors and lawyers and stuff, they're all healthy …

Shut up! You're not going to persuade me! You're not going to rationalize me into doing this!

But it wasn't just some force of morality that I was arguing with, it was the Bonk. And when the Bonk is angry, it must be appeased.

A few meters later, I was bending to the ground to scavenge my first packet. I put it to my lips, not caring who I was sharing it with. I squeezed and produced a pea-sized morsel of GU.

The line had been crossed, and from that moment on I hardly traversed a foot without picking up at least one or two used packets.

It was distasteful business, but bit by bit, my strength returned. No doubt I would have finished running the entire marathon that way. But suddenly, I saw it!

My final salvation!

The ultimate Bonk killer!

There, on the pavement, glowing brightly under a single beam of light shining straight from heaven, virtually untouched: a Power Bar with only a tiny nibble taken from the upper left corner.

I sprinted forward like a hyena pouncing on a baby gazelle. In my madness, I was fearful that some other Bonking madman would stoop to claim the prize. Predictably, the dash to the discarded Power Bar was a one-horse race. I skidded to a halt and reached down to grab the relic and clutch it to my chest. The sun had warmed it to the perfect temperature, it had been baking in the midday heat for who knows how long. In a flash, I ripped open the shiny, golden wrapper and stuffed the whole nutrient wad into my mouth, nearly losing a finger in the process. A Power Bar never tasted so good.

I lumbered awkwardly to the finish. The Bonk scurried back into its dark and lonely hole.

Defeating the Bonk lacks dignity I suppose, but dignity's got nothing to do with survival. After all, isn't that why we do silly things like marathons? Isn't that why we push ourselves, why we train, why we sweat and suffer? Don't we want to discover where our limits are and then exceed them?

I know I do.

But then again, it brings to mind something Hunter S. Thompson once said.

"The Edge... there is no honest way to explain it because the only people who really know where it is are the ones who have gone over."

Amen, brother, amen!

Actually, when you come to think of it, maybe I am

smart enough to avoid the Bonk. Maybe I allow it to take me from time to time?

Maybe there's a certain amount of comfort in every now and then coming face to face with the feral animal that we all carry inside.

The call of the wild might not be pretty, but it's true.

The Bonk is dead—long live the Bonk!

CHAPTER 31

With the ski team humming along and my body finally in decent form, it was time for the real traveling to begin. I'd already been to Australia, so I wasn't necessarily a novice when it came to international escapade, but there was still quite a bit of the world to see, and if skiing could be the motivating factor to get the ball rolling, then that was all the better.

The next big step for me as a traveler/skier was to spend some time in non-English-speaking countries. I got word from Kathryn that she and her family were headed to Europe to do two Worldloppet races and I jumped at the chance to join them. The races they were doing were the Marcialonga in Italy, which runs from Moena to Cavalese; and the Konig Ludwig Lauf in Oberammergau, Germany. The trip would involve planes, trains, automobiles and, of course, skis. In addition to Kathryn and her family there would be another American coming, a retired gentleman named Bob Vangene. Bob was famous for being number four on the list of Worldloppet masters. He was a feisty guy who stormed through the races like … the Terminator.

Plans were made, tickets were bought, and before I knew it I was up in the air and on my way.

Going to Europe isn't like crossing state borders or even going to Canada. In light of my experience traveling to Australia I had learned to cherish my passport like it was a guardian angel. In a way, the whole trip felt more like an expedition than a vacation.

My adventures are always influenced by the fact that I don't like to plan in advance. I find that you can turn a totally mundane undertaking into a desperate struggle for survival simply by approaching it unprepared and overconfident. Needless to say, this philosophy has got a couple holes in it.

I have to admit that I felt no small amount of trepidation as I stepped off the plane in Frankfurt and realized the full implications of not speaking a word of German or Italian, or any other language besides English. My first sensations were weakness and vulnerability. The idea of exposing myself to the extreme physical exhaustion of two ski marathons under such a mindset was a bit daunting.

Luckily for me, my companions didn't share my general traveling philosophies and I was continually amazed at how much organization they had managed to achieve two months prior to departure and from more than a thousand miles away. You can't plan everything, however, and I hoped that my off-the-cuff experience would smooth enough roadblocks along the way that I wouldn't feel entirely like a freeloader.

I tagged along with our international group to a fabulous

little bed and breakfast in Moena, Italy, which—with further kudos to the preparation of my companions—was near the Marcialonga starting area. In fact, the course went through the parking lot of the establishment. The place was bustling with friendly skiers, all of them continually performing bizarre surgery on their skis with unidentifiable equipment and unfathomable purpose. They were cheerful, though, and would repeatedly run off to fetch our single hostess who spoke a little broken English in order to translate their eager, endless questions. When her language skills failed her, we resorted to sign language and crude drawings. We had many pleasant conversations that were in no small way attributable to the fact that we couldn't understand each other in the least.

I quickly found it was good having Bob along since, being surrounded by people of other nations, it was up to us to extol the greatness of the United States—plus we took great mischievous pleasure in antagonizing the Australians. I remember one occasion when I tried to get everyone in our group to pay me a quarter for looking at the, according to me, American-owned moon—it's got our flag on it after all. Somebody told me about some international law against moon ownership. I responded that such an idea was absurd.

All joking aside, back then and probably even today, you sometimes end up being a bit of an American apologist when engaging in international travel. America is just like any other country in the world in that it has had its triumphant moments and it has had its lesser moments and it has had every kind of moment in between. It's a better philosophy to measure a country by the average whole rather than focus on the peaks and valleys, but that doesn't stop a massive percentage of people from doing the exact opposite.

In the end, people are people. When you have finally traveled enough, you realize that we're fundamentally not all that different.

However in my early journeys I hadn't learned that yet, and I sometimes got into silly arguments.

There was one time when I was hiking down a street in Moena trying, and failing, to successfully convince the Australians why private citizens should have the right to own handguns, I am from Wisconsin, after all. For the record, my argument was that banning handguns wasn't about saving lives since automobiles kill a lot more people than handguns do on a yearly basis and nobody ever talked about banning them, a silly argument of course, but I was sticking by it. Anyway, the conversation quickly deteriorated into an America thing, and Bob, being the elder statesman, was always granted the floor when he spoke up to make a point.

I had been feeling on the verge of being overrun when Bob offered his most essential position on the U.S. To this day I haven't forgotten what he said.

"Well," he sighed with the word "America" floating in the air at the end of a half-finished thought, "it's a lousy, lousy, lousy, lousy country."

He paused and took two steps as my heart sank in defeat. But then he finished with a, resonant coda.

"But it's still the best one!"

The words were so chipper and matter-of-fact that we couldn't help but disintegrate into absurd laughter—at least I did.

Since then, I have found that it's quite common for people to name the country they're from as the best in the world which speaks well to the global level of individual satisfaction when you think about it. Personally, I wouldn't have that any other way.

A few days later we had forgotten all about our political disagreements as we prepared to make our way through Italy's incomparable seventy-kilometer ski event, the Marcialonga.

We trained on the course in the days preceding the race. It's a wonderful trail that runs along a river at the bottom of a beautiful mountain valley. The pine-covered mountains rise on either side and frame the whole community in such pastoral perfection that it would be difficult to imagine a more perfect setting for cross-country skiing.

The villages scattered along the course are the types you'd expect to see in a snow globe. They're haphazard and ancient with the roads presumably coming as an afterthought to the placement of the structures. This causes the highways and byways to branch off in an incomprehensible lattice that spreads through the town like tree roots.

The inherent chaos of the city layouts added a tremendous amount of character to the ambiance, but it also made it confusing to get around.

The villages themselves are composed of cute buildings made from wood and stone that seem more like the miniature country cottages you'd find in a collectibles shop than real places of habitation. We were a little confused by the fact that the Marcialonga trail seemed to simply end at the outskirts of these towns, forcing us to walk through to the other side, where it resumed again. It was a bit of a mystery how the organizers planned to take us through these communities since there never seemed to be a single straightforward route, but we would have to wait until the actual race to see how this obstacle was handled.

On race morning, we got up early and managed to beg a simple bowl of oatmeal from our gourmet-minded hosts before skiing down to the start of the event. It was a beautiful mild day, the kind where a lightweight Lycra ski suit is almost too warm.

It wasn't until I shed my warm-ups and stood shivering in the starting area that I realized something about this race was different. There was a feeling of excitement in the air, the kind of excitement you normally only experience in the final few desperate seconds preceding the gun. But it was already prevalent here a full fifteen minutes before the start. I remembered wondering how they did it, how could the participants maintain this level of eagerness? I just giggled and shook my head. It wouldn't be the last time I'd do it that day.

Standing on a starting line and looking down the barrel of a seventy-kilometer event is traumatizing enough. Add the fact that you don't speak a word of the language of the region and that you don't know exactly how you're going to get back to your hotel afterwards and it becomes downright surreal. I just stood there scanning vibrant, eager, faces that flashed with glee and bounced with anticipation. They know how to party in Italy, and they were ready to get going.

By the time the gun finally went off, my fellow competitors had worked themselves up to such a volatile state that we hardly managed to go fifteen yards before we all collapsed into the most spectacular crash I've ever had the privilege to be a part of. Bodies, poles and skis flailed to the melodious sound of a thousand voices cursing in Italian. I joined in eagerly with my own favorite vulgarities which, although probably not understood, were embraced as befitting the atmosphere. It felt like a kind of initiation, which I passed because I sprang up smiling like all the rest.

We tore off across the wicked-fast track and hit the first town in grand, fast, fashion. I was shocked to discover that the officials had solved the route placement problem by simply paving every road in the town with a blanket of snow. Everywhere you looked there were lines of skiers skittering up alleyways and traveling in every conceivable direction. On top of that, it was as if the whole town was animated for the event. Spectators hung out windows or perched on top of walls, vigorously clanging cow bells or yelling at the top of their voices. I was so disoriented, I just focused on the skier in front of me, hoping he knew where he was going, but also wishing I could just stop and soak it all in.

In short order, we were out of the village and heading toward the river. The course goes slightly uphill for the first twenty kilometers, followed by thirty-five kilometers on a gradual descent and ending with a brutal fifteen-kilometer climb to the top of the framing mountains and the finish at Cavalese. The trail was a surprise at every turn, sometimes narrowing to a few feet wide, other times expanding to several hundred meters. The river wound along beside the trail, and at one point it reared up at the bottom of a massive, icy hill the specter of which didn't deter any of my competitors in the least. I was terrified because it was so hard to cut an edge into that hard surface that I thought I was going to end up in the water. As I used every means in my power to control my speed, skiers shot by on either side, some crashing magnificently, others simply flashing dashing grins and laughing encouragement.

We continued up and then down the river. I looked forward to every town along the way for the excitement of the spectators and the novelty of skiing down streets and sidewalks. One missed turn sent me through a narrow chute at an incredible speed. In order to avoid the wall at the bottom I had to fling myself into such a desperately sharp turn that I stayed upright only by slamming my hand into the snow and using it as a pivot. I laughed out loud after that one—gripped by a sensation of pure euphoria.

People lined the whole course, yelling and laughing like no other race I've ever been in. Most of them carried starting lists so they could reference our numbers and scream our names as we came by. The race evaporated all too fast as the hours seemed to pass by in a rush.

The last hill was an absolute fiend. We trudged up, exhausted by the previous fifty kilometers but also thankful for the hill's length because it slowed down the pace and allowed us to soak in the moments. At the top, one final crazy dash through a groomed mountain town preceded the finish line. The crowd was larger there than at any other point along the trail and they welcomed every finisher with unparalleled and undiminished excitement.

I wandered around for a while with that sort of happy, zoned-out feeling you always get at the end of a race. Somehow I managed to get the coveted stamp in my Worldloppet passport and find my gear bag. It was while I was changing into my dry clothes that I noticed skiers emerging from a tent with strange Styrofoam containers. Curious, I staggered over only to discover that they were handing out spaghetti. A skier's fantasy come true! I received my generous helping and chowed down with the kind of ravenous abandon that only skiers are familiar with. I had seventy kilometers' worth of refueling to do and I worked on that saucy, spicy, wonderful entree for what seemed like a blissful eternity. Yet, and this is the part that I still don't believe, when I finally had to admit I had eaten as much as I possibly could, I gazed back into the bowl and it looked as if it had hardly been touched.

Surely it was some sort of Styrofoam horn-of-plenty, magically connected to the divine spaghetti pot in the sky.

In a daze, I made it back to my hotel for the rendezvous with my other travel companions. I can assure you we slept soundly and contentedly after our Marcialonga experience. That was one of those rare days you remember forever, where everything goes even better than you could have hoped.

Now, I love all our Wisconsin area races purely and absolutely. I'm anxious all summer long because the hot days make our pristine winter ski trails seem like vague and wispy dreams. But as much as I appreciate the conditions and the events held locally, I have to admit, if there was some way that I could be in Italy every winter for the Marcialonga, I'd do it without a second thought. The Marcialonga is the most amazing race you can imagine.

Oberammergau was a great experience as well. We stayed at a youth hostel and spent our free time before the race heading out to various tourist attractions like Mad King Ludwig's castle. King Ludwig is the figure for which the Konig Ludwig Lauf is named and he's internationally famous for having built the castle that Walt Disney used as inspiration for the castle at the gates of Disney World and for the Disney logo. If you ever get a chance to go to Oberammergau and check it out, you'll be stunned. This isn't a case of "inspiration" so much as a case of "blatant rip-off."

I thought I was going to be exhausted after having skied the Marcialonga so recently, but that race had been predominantly downhill, and I felt surprisingly good at Oberammergau. The course wound its way through thick, black German forests and there were moments when the ski trail meandered around the gentle curves of frozen rivers. It was subdued and relaxing after the exuberant Marcialonga, and it was also a fantastic event.

Writing this now, fifteen years later, the details I remember are that one of the women in our group objected to the fact that the female bibs had "dame" stamped on them. She was under the impression that "dame" was a derogatory term. I was finally able to calm her down a little bit when I explained that the word wasn't meant to be said with the English pronunciation, which rhymes with "game," but should be spoken with the German pronunciation, two syllables, like "Dharma" without the "r."

"It's the German word for 'lady,'" I said.

She was appeased if not satisfied.

The other thing I remember was that at a food station I reached for a glass of what I thought was lime Gatorade that turned out to be chicken noodle soup. It's quite a shock to the system when you're preparing your body for something sweet only to have the taste you encounter be overwhelmingly salty.

Finishing all the races was an emotional as well as physical marathon. It's amazing the confidence that surges through you after you've successfully navigated a foreign culture, language, and terrain; not to mention having completed the physical challenge of the races.

It was honestly one of the greatest trips of my life.

There was one minor black spot that I'm embarrassed to reveal.

The month and year of this trip was January 1997. For those who live in Wisconsin, January 1997 is revered as the month and year the Green Bay Packers won their record-extending twelfth NFL Championship and third Super Bowl.

Many in Wisconsin will probably be able to tell you exactly where they were on January 26 when the Lombardi trophy came home. I can sure tell you where I was … in a quaint and beautiful bed and breakfast in Moena, Italy, THAT DIDN'T HAVE A TV!

To make matters worse, because of the time difference, the game was in the middle of the night. So there I was, the day after the Marcialonga, wandering the streets of Moena looking for a place with a cable feed to the U.S.

I'm sad to say my efforts were unsuccessful.

I went back to my room a defeated man, hoping that I would be able to avoid any media outlet until the end of the trip so that I might be able to "experience" the game on tape without having the result spoiled for me.

I eventually did watch it at home, and found that most of the joy of a Super Bowl win comes from experiencing the satisfied glow of the residents of the victorious state. That, at least, was something I could surround myself with for a whole year.

In Moena, Kathryn had a funny moment when she tried

to ask an Italian policeman if he knew what the score of the Super Bowl was. The fellow bustled off and chatted with his colleagues for a few minutes behind some closed doors before returning with a piece of paper with a crudely scrawled score.

"35-21," it said.

"Well, who won?" Kathryn asked.

The policeman looked at her like she was daft.

"It's obvious who won," he grunted gesturing at the paper. "The team that scored thirty-five!"

Fortunately I did get to watch Aaron Rodgers lead the Packers to championship number 13 in February of 2011, so missing the game in 97' isn't so painful anymore.

CHAPTER 32

As the years went on, I continued to notch my ski pole with Birkies and marathons. The dates would click by on the calendar and every year I'd find myself in the same place with the same people doing the same thing. The race calendar doesn't change, but doing the events year after year establishes a line of continuity through your life that adds another magnificent dimension to the Birkie experience. It's a dimension that causes a distinct shift of perspective over time.

Bit by bit, I began to understand that the quality of my individual race could never be as important as the simple act of participation. I learned to relax and enjoy the ride no matter if I didn't finish as fast as I thought I was capable of, or as high on the result list, or even ahead of my friendly rivals from the smaller, local races. The simple, positive sense of collective consciousness that comes through the repetition of these events over decades is a more enticing goal to pursue. I'd done races fast and slow, starting at the front and at the back, in good fitness and in poor; and I found that the line between myself and the other competitors had started to blur. It no longer felt like a competition. Instead, I could empathize with everyone who simply had the courage to be out there. After all, at the end of the day, we all run the same race.

But even with all my efforts to grow into a more positive attitude, there was still the occasional situation that piqued my irritation.

One of my most memorable moments of annoyance came not at a Birkie, but at the end of an exceptionally brutal Grandma's marathon. One of my college friends, William Cross had come along to make some noise for me. It was an occupation he engaged with exceptional fortitude, and for which I remain heartily grateful.

Grandma's was especially difficult that year. Even when you're in fairly good shape, you occasionally have a downer of a race that takes you an hour or so longer than you expected. Sometimes you're a little bit ill, sometimes you're over-trained, and other times you just aren't at the level you believed yourself to be. Any number of things can have a radical negative effect on your performance.

That particular year, the problem was the heat. Throughout the last ten kilometers or so, people were really suffering. I remember seeing one woman who was dressed all in black suddenly go wobbly and collapse into the arms of a confused spectator.

These things happen during marathons. But thankfully I survived without any lasting hardship, although not in a time I was about to brag about.

After the race, I was sitting in the passenger's seat of

William's car with no more life in me than you would find in a runny egg.

"Wow! That was great!" William cried with typical enthusiasm, "You did awesome!"

"Thanks," I replied dejectedly. I was not in the frame of mind to take compliments right then. Instead, I slouched down into the car seat and tried to drift off into sleep.

"Hey, you want to stop off at the beach and skip stones for a while?"

The suggestion actually caused an icy chill to run down my spine. The absurdity of somebody asking me to go and skip stones while I was completely and utterly spent was almost too much to process. It wasn't so much the suggestion itself that was inappropriate, it was the obliviousness it indicated. William had demonstrated himself to be utterly unaware of my pitiful physical state and I was worried about what other psychotic endeavors he might have in mind. In fact, it was entirely possible that in comparison to the other "fun" activities he'd been contemplating, pitching the skipping stones idea was a show of remarkable restraint.

However, I decided not to succumb to annoyance and instead tried to keep things in perspective. I was still eternally grateful that he was driving me home and I had to remember that the day was just starting for him, whereas for me it was irrevocably over. Somehow I was going to have to make him understand that.

"I kind of need to sleep."

"Oh, yeah, I suppose."

We continued to drive along. All I could think about was my bed, lying in my bed, sleeping in my bed, forgetting the pain in my legs and the headache in my mind. I was fried.

Fortunately, it wasn't that long of a drive. I laid back and shut my eyes. We'd be there in no time.

After a little while, something disturbed me. Somehow the car didn't feel right. I cracked open an eyelid and had a look outside. Vehicles where whizzing past us. I looked at William's speedometer; it read 45 miles an hour.

"Hey man," I croaked, "you're only going 45."

"Yeah, I like to save a little on gas."

I bit my lip in an attempt not to say anything. Four hundred yards went by. I couldn't take it.

"Could you pick it up a little bit? I really need to get home and get to bed. I feel terrible."

"Oh, yeah man, of course."

I felt the seat surge beneath me as we accelerated. All was right in the world. We'd be home soon now, blessed sleep, blessed relaxation, blessed … wait a minute. It felt like the car was slowing down again.

I cracked open my eyes.

We *were* slowing down.

In fact, we were stopping.

"Uhhhhh … ." I said, which was as much a query as it was threat. At least I hoped it was.

"Hey man, look at that big snapping turtle!" William cried.

I glanced forward. Indeed, there was a huge snapping turtle in the middle of the road. It was lumbering slowly along on some undoubtedly vital quest.

"Dude, that thing's got to be fifty years old!" William continued happily.

William was a biologist. He was possessed by a childlike excitement every time he saw something alive and primordial.

"It's great," I replied, "can we go home now? I've seen snapping turtles before."

But William was captivated and concerned.

"He's right out in the middle of the road, somebody's going to hit him. That would be a tragedy."

"Nonsense," I replied, yawning. "He got to be fifty didn't he? He knows what he's doing, don't worry about it."

"Nope, I've got to do something, I've got to get him off the road."

To William, this had become a matter of civic duty to human civilization and Mother Nature. He started searching frantically in his car for a pair of gloves or something he could use to urge the turtle along. I began to grow concerned.

"Actually, snapping turtles can be a bit dangerous," I said. "They bite you and … "

"Oh, I won't let it bite me."

"But … "

"Nonsense."

"But they can jump up in the air and … "

Slam! The car door shut.

I was talking to an empty seat.

Weakly, I stared out the window as my friend approached the primitive reptile. The turtle was huge, about the size of an adult English bulldog. William had chosen his ice scraper as an encouraging device. It was one of those long ice scrapers with a nylon brush on one end.

Cars whizzed past.

The turtle looked like something out of the Cretaceous period. Its armor was miniature spiny pyramids that interlinked across its back.

The image that repeatedly flashed through my mind like a blood-drenched slasher film was the snapping turtle springing twelve feet through the air to chomp down on William's exposed jugular with its death grip. Such an attack would require me, in my weakened state, to drag William's body, with the turtle still attached, to the car, somehow get them both inside, and go like a madman to the nearest hospital.

I sighed.

I held my breath.

The turtle's hind legs began to tighten.

I watched as my friend slowly approached his imminent doom.

Closer.

Closer.

Closer.

The turtle gazed up, its ancient, beady eyes glinting with swamp rage.

I knew with certainty that this situation was simply too absurd for any of us to survive.

The ice scraper tapped the turtle's cartilaginous shell.

I expected the beast to snap like a mouse trap ... but nothing happened.

The turtle just sat there dumbly. Apparently the things people had told me about snapping turtles and their fierce jumping ability had been greatly exaggerated. In fact, the turtle looked rather awkward as it started to rumble and move. It was no task at all for William to maneuver himself around behind it, and from there it was an easy matter to simply start whacking the beast encouragingly on the tail with the scraper to keep it moving. The snapper began to high-step it across the road like a child walking across a hot, sandy beach. Its knees leaped up like Deion Sanders returning an interception, only in super-slow motion. Every now and then, when its progress slowed, William found it necessary to rain a couple of unceasing blows on the beast's head. The turtle took them in annoyance, squinting its already squinty eyes and bowing its tortured brow.

It was the most preposterous thing I'd ever seen.

Cars continued to fly by, many of them blaring their horns in annoyance.

My legs hurt.

The car was hot.

I was miserable.

Suddenly, I started to laugh. It was just too ridiculous. It's in bizarre moments like those that you're sometimes granted a little bit of perspective into just how tiny and pathetic most daily problems really are. Just because I'd decided on that particular day to put myself through an exorbitant physical challenge didn't mean that I really had the right to put my wants or desires over the needs of a primitive creature that was probably twenty-five years my senior. Doing the marathon been my choice, hadn't it? I could just have easily decided to stay in bed and drink a milkshake rather than run 26.2 miles. The pain was part of the consequences.

The turtle continued to crawl along.

William stood behind him, incessantly urging it on its way.

And that's when it occurred to me that the whole stupid image was a perfect representation of the events of the day and for every race. The competitors are the turtles. The spectators are the motivators. Neither is complete without the other, and once your attention's been drawn to it, it's really not all that hard to put aside your petty annoyances, and recognize the importance of the whole.

I relaxed, leaned against the window, and resolved to show a little bit more appreciation and understanding for the people who came out to cheer in my corner.

It was a resolution I maintained even through successive stops to save a starving coyote, rescue a wounded bald eagle, and untangle an entwined porcupine. But, I have to admit, by the time we got to the epileptic moose, I was starting to get annoyed again.

CHAPTER 33

With Grandma's behind me, I felt that I had some unfinished business down in Australia. I had been extremely dissatisfied with my first performance in the Hoppet, so I made the ridiculous sacrifices that it takes to escape reality and voyage down under for a month of cross-country skiing. Most people don't do trips like that because they're afraid of quitting their jobs, or getting a fifth mortgage, or selling a kidney for financing the journey. Fortunately I had my priorities in order.

It was with some surprise that I again found myself staggering out of the Melbourne airport after a solid thirty hours of travel several months after my initial, meager preparations. The airplane food hadn't killed me and neither had the movies *Dante's Peak* or *101 Dalmatians*, though I had been tempted to walk out on both of them. Again I felt like a first-class fool standing in that parking lot with my ski bag on a day that was about four hundred degrees too hot for snow.

Ethan and Kathryn were there to meet me, and almost

instantly we were making the winding, nauseating drive up to Lake Mountain. There, up in the gum-tree covered Australian altitude, hidden away among the clouds, we found the glorious hard-packed trails that only a skier knows how to gaze upon and call beautiful. It felt really good to get on snow again and after I'd had at it a while and was starting to get my form back, Ethan suggested that I ski the Australian nationals. His logic was that they would be the best-organized races in the country, and it is kind of hard to dig up a ski race down there under normal circumstances. He also thought I would be good enough to avoid embarrassing myself and, as a perk, I would get to see Anthony Evans, Australia's national champion, in action. I figured they were mostly interval starts and I like interval starts, so I decided what the heck!

As a first-wave Birkie skier, I was kind of hoping that at the very worst I would be competent enough to stay out of the way of the best racers. I also thought it would be interesting to see how good the world-class guys really are. It was exciting to hear Ethan talk about Anthony Evans. He's been an Olympian and at World Cup events and had done about as well as the top Americans. I guess you could say he was among the world's top thirty or forty skiers at the time. In Australia, however, he was a champion and had won the nationals for the last four years and was bringing a streak of eighteen consecutive nationals victories into that year's event. The record was twenty-one consecutive victories and Anthony was the odds-on favorite to take the title by winning all four of the upcoming races.

The first race was a fifteen-kilometer skate race in New South Wales at the Perisher Valley. On the way, we passed through the site of the tragic Thredbo landslide that had occurred just a few days before. I remember watching the news as they dug a young man out of a horrible tangle of rubble. The landslide had hit at night while he had been sleeping next to his wife. Though they had been in the same bed, he had survived and, tragically, she hadn't.

Sometimes your fate is determined by something as simple as which side of the bed you choose to sleep on. That, if nothing else, should illustrate how little control over life people really have.

Our path took us on a road that went right through the site. They had the disaster area fenced off, forcing us to detour around but we could still see the affected area pretty clearly. It didn't seem as big as one would have imagined after having seen so many images of the area on television, but it seemed to be ten times more horrible than the media had reported.

When we arrived at Perisher, it was snowing really hard, which is always a pleasant surprise in Australia. We weren't able to ski the course like we had been planning on because the weather was so bad, but when we went back down the mountain to our rooms, we found about four inches of new snow there as well. That was unbelievably unusual so everybody got all excited and we skied around in a small circle until it was pretty well packed down. Then we did some sprints around it for a while before turning in for our beauty rest. I think in our excitement we might have worked ourselves a little too hard.

The next day was really nice and sunny and we were excited to go out for the race. We got there early enough to do a long warm-up and decided to do a loop of the course. It was a five-kilometer loop, the men had to do three laps and the women only one. I wasn't too far into my warm-up when I realized I was in for a long day. I think M.C. Escher designed the course because even though it started and finished at the same spot, it just kept going up and up without a single downhill. I sort of anticipated a nationals race to be difficult, but man, that was brutal. The snow didn't help, either, they had groomed what had fallen the night before but the base wasn't all that firm.

At the gun I did my best, but the combination of altitude and soft base caused me to struggle dearly. As I methodically trudged along, I heard the scattered spectators behind me get excited, so I turned around to see Anthony Evans himself bearing down on me. I was a little intimidated and, not wanting to ruin the chances of a guy who had the potential to win a national race, I jumped completely off the track. As he came by I was sort of shocked to hear him politely call out "Thanks!" He was whipping his poles back and forth so fast they were making a whooshing sound. Later, we joked that he probably had the time to stop, have a conversation with me, and then go on to win. We also tried to re-create the sound of his poles, but failed.

Predictably, Anthony was the first Australian, coming in at about forty-five minutes. The best in the race was an international competitor form Korea. That made nineteen consecutive nationals victories for Anthony with another race in a week.

Next up was a thirty-kilometer skate race at Falls Creek in Victoria, which made us happy since it was a much shorter drive from Melbourne than it was to Perisher. As I've mentioned before, Falls Creek is where they hold the Kangaroo Hoppet and is probably the best place to cross-country ski in Australia.

You'd think that with forty-two kilometers of trails available, they would be able to set up a course without laps, but no. We had to do six laps of a five-kilometer course because that was the only way they could make it hard enough. It was darn difficult, too, all up and then one massive, ridiculously steep downhill with a sharp turn at the bottom, which provided no reprieve whatsoever. There was no flat area to speak of.

We did a practice run on the race course the day before and after the Perisher race I was a little worried that maybe I wouldn't hold up very well. But it's good to be concerned before a race because that means it's important to you and you're going to try your hardest. My goal with this race was to not get lapped, which was actually quite an ambitious undertaking considering the level of competition. In addition to Australia's best skiers, there were also a couple of junior skiers from Sweden at this event. Like a fool, I failed to write down their names. It's a shame because they are probably both gold medalists by now.

I set about doing my six laps and came to especially

hate a particular wall of a hill in the middle of the course. As I approached the end of lap number five, I started to hope my dream of not being lapped might actually come true. But then I heard the telltale sounds of excitement at the sight of Anthony coming up behind me again.

I looked up and realized I was very close to the finish area and that perhaps I could sprint and make it to the turn off before they captured me, but instead I opted to jump off the trail again. I was just a guest in these races after all, and the thought of being the one responsible for a crash that screwed up the chances of a contender was simply terrifying.

Standing beside the course, I marveled at Anthony and the two Swedes. Again, although he was in a dog fight, Anthony had time to shout, "Thanks!" politely. Anthony Evans was an easy guy to like.

I watched them finish and then headed out on my final lap. Anthony was once again the first Australian although one of the Swedes was the overall winner. That made twenty victories with one more to go for the tie.

That race more than any other gave me a real appreciation for how good those top guys are. No matter how hard you think you're training, there's always another level you can aspire to. The dedication of an Olympic-class athlete is beyond belief. There would be days when I'd see the national team members doing hill repeats without poles on the steepest hill they could find. Then, later in the day, you might see them going on a mountain bike ride below the snowline or going for a run. They are so committed, it's hard to feel at all bothered when they fly by you. It's almost as though the price of their speed is too high.

The next two races were classic technique, a ten-kilometer and a fifteen-kilometer, both of which were held at Falls Creek. I really didn't expect to do well in them because I'd just bought my classic skis the previous December so my technique was still pretty awful. Having been just barely respectable in the skating races, I was just hoping to avoid embarrassment.

The course for the classic race was again laps, this time with only one shocking uphill and a bit more flat area. Perhaps they thought they had worked us hard enough. I took off with the gun and managed to finish without crashing or running into anybody. I wasn't great, but I didn't finish last, so I was satisfied.

Anthony got the shocker—for the first time in nearly five years, he didn't win a nationals race. Fellow Australian Paul Gray finished nine seconds ahead of him. Anthony is a pretty humble champion and he took it very well, being careful not to take any of the spotlight from Paul at the awards ceremony.

I was given a nice certificate of participation along with all the other international skiers. One of the other Swedish juniors was the first across the line. Those kids were awesome.

Anthony Evans had just missed out on equaling the Australian mark of twenty-one consecutive national victories and I think he may have been a little irritated about that.

The day of the last race was wicked. It was windy and snowy and nobody knew how to wax for kick. We were all standing around at the start with fifteen minutes left to go with absolutely nothing that worked. Everybody was going out on test skis and trying to find something with little success. Finally, I threw on some Swix purple and carried my skis to the starting line. I figured there was no point in seeing if they gripped or not, I didn't have any other waxes to try. They counted down and I was off double-poling up the first little hill. I was afraid to try to kick because I thought it would be embarrassing to fall flat on my face in front of everybody if my wax didn't bite. Finally, when I was a little more out of sight, I gave a kick. Nothing happened. I felt a little twinge of panic when I considered that now I would have to double-pole the whole fifteen kilometers, but then I just resigned myself to it and kept on.

The wind was brutal and really cold. Out on top of a mountain like Falls Creek, it's awfully exposed; the chunks of ice and snow really sting as they drive into your face.

I was feeling worse and worse until I started going up a small hill and discovered that somehow, magically, I had acquired some kick. The same wind that was making me so miserable was blowing the loose snow into the icy track and that stuff functioned pretty well with the wax I had on. My spirits lifted quite a bit and though my skis were balling up pretty badly at the finish, I thought I might get a good result because I presumed my wax had been more effective than most of the competitors.

Anthony Evans didn't have any problem with the wax,

apparently. He flew around that course, winning first Australian over Paul Gray by about two minutes with a several-second overall victory to boot. All of the people in my little group of friends were frustrated because Anthony's great race dropped our percentage behind the winner way back. I was disappointed, too, because I thought I had raced better than the day before but I had dropped in comparison to Anthony. Still, I was encouraged when I saw I had improved in comparison to Ben Derrick, who is another member of the Australian national team. Ben eventually went on to win the Kangaroo Hoppet multiple times.

An overall victory for the national champion Anthony Evans was a very appropriate way for the nationals to conclude. I was pretty happy to have them done, whatever the results. There were a lot of great athletes there and it was an honor to be able to ski with them. My perspective had changed a lot. It's hard to appreciate how hard Olympic-caliber athletes work until you have toed the line beside them and then limped to the finish several days later.

You know though, it's not at all discouraging. Just to be around an event like that and see firsthand what it is like at the elite level is really inspiring. You think you train hard all year and then you see that people are out there doing three times as much as you do. It's hard to believe that people can put so much of themselves into one thing.

I finished the race season by having a great race at the Kangaroo Hoppet and finishing thirty-third overall.

In many ways, the Hoppet felt like an extension of the Australian national championships. The same guys were numbers one through thirty-two just as they had been in every nationals event. Australia is a small enough skiing community that you feel like you're elite because you are constantly rubbing elbows with the guys who actually are.

At the end of the Hoppet, some kids even ran up to me and asked for my autograph. I'm sure they were disappointed later when they looked me up and found that I was a nobody, but who knows, maybe someday I'll do something significant that makes those autographs worth something.

CHAPTER 34

Feeling inspired by the athletes I'd seen in Australia, I decided to push my ski training up another notch. In the back of my mind, I was hoping that I could make the jump from the first wave to the "elite" wave of the Birkie, and for that I'd have to finish within the top two hundred skiers.

I'd seen Australia's national team do a lot of hill-bounding, and I thought that was exactly what I needed to gain more speed and strength. Cross-country skiing is all about the uphills after all, and the more you focus specifically on climbing, the faster you're going to get.

Hill-bounding is exactly what it sounds like. You find a big hill and run or "bound" up it, doing your best to approximate your skiing technique. If you're running on an unpaved road or trail, you can use your regular ski poles, but if you're running on a paved road you need to switch the snow baskets to road ferrules just like you do with roller-skiing. As with roller-skiing, I wouldn't recommend using the best and lightest ski poles that you own for hill-bounding. A truly great pair of ski poles can cost you a couple hundred dollars and you don't need to risk wear and tear on that equipment for fall and summer training.

With my mind made up to do some hill-bounding, the next thing to do was find an appropriate place to train. Believe it or not, it's actually not all that easy to discover a good long, steep hill to run up and down. Most highway road crews do a pretty good job of bulldozing flat all the local hills for the streets they make. You wouldn't want to train on a major highway anyway because it's always better to get yourself out of the direct pathway of speeding vehicles.

I racked my brain trying to think of a good hill somewhere and finally remembered a bike ride that I had done through Elk Mound. Bike rides are great in that you end up discovering hundreds of quaint and wonderful things about the place where you live that you would never have noticed if you'd only observed your community through the windows of your car.

Sometime back I'd happened to ride through Elk Mound and I had discovered a long hill in Elk Mound Village Park. The hill is a paved road that rises up to an observation tower known as Mound Hill Park Castle. To call it a "castle" is a bit of an exaggeration since it's essentially a tower, but I have to admit that the view from the top is quite spectacular.

It wasn't the tower that interested me so much as the hill leading up to it, and since it was only a fifteen-minute drive from my apartment, I realized it was the perfect place for ski training.

Destination in mind, the only thing I lacked was some

poor soul to drag along with me on another one of my crazy adventures. My thoughts quickly turned to my friend William Cross, who was still going to school in the area. I knew William had a touch of Birkie fever that I thought needed to be magnified.

I dialed his number eagerly.

"Hey William, I've got a plan for us!"

"Oh no, what now!"

"Have you done a workout yet today?"

"No," he said, and then made a kind of resigned sigh as if he instantly regretted his honesty.

"Great, we're going hill-bounding!"

"Hill-whatting?"

"Just put on your running gear, get some gloves, grab some ski poles, and meet me in twenty minutes."

I slammed down the phone before he could protest and laughed to myself. Someday I hope some fanatical individual calls me up and demands that I be ready in twenty minutes with a random list of bizarre items without offering any further indication as to what's in store.

Twenty minutes later, I loaded William into my car and fifteen minutes after that we were standing at the bottom of the Elk Mound Observatory hill.

"What are we going to do?" William asked.

"We're going to run up this."

"Really? With poles?"

"Yeah," I said, and I showed him how you can run

while simultaneously propelling yourself forward with your ski poles, mimicking the stride of a classical skier. It really only works when you're running uphill, since when you're running on a flat you go too fast for the poles to be of any use.

"Ahhh," William said, still not convinced. He seemed to be about to protest more, so I decided to deflect that impending argument with the pull of competition.

"I'll meet you at the top. Go!"

I hit my watch and started sprinting up the hill.

The thing about doing any kind of interval workout is that you always want to go at the maximum possible effort for the duration of the interval. The idea is that you're trying to artificially create a mini-race to train your body how to be efficient under such conditions. You want to teach your lungs and muscles to be able to sustain the highest possible effort for the longest possible time. The problem most people have, especially on their first interval, is that they tend to go too hard and burn out before they can finish the distance.

I had been up the Elk Mound hill a couple of times on a bike and in a car, but there is nothing that prepares you for running or hill-bounding up a particular obstacle. You simply don't know what the obstacle is like until you've run it. I didn't even have an idea how long it was going to take me to get to the top of the hill, so I didn't exactly know how to pace myself.

The result was that I went out way too fast and got myself

into difficulty within about a minute of the start. It's hard to slow down and recover during an interval, but I had no other choice than to reduce my pace and try to concentrate on breathing for a little while. Behind me I heard William's poles clacking against the pavement interspersed with his labored breathing and cursing.

After plodding along for a while, I was able to crank it up again to an appropriate effort level and finish off the hill. Hitting my watch at the top, I was surprised to discover that the hill took a good six minutes to run. Although that might not have been a long enough interval for an Olympic-caliber athlete, it was a very acceptable amount of time for me.

A few minutes later, William came huffing and panting to the end.

"This is craziness," he puffed as he tried to regain his breath, but I could tell he secretly liked it.

"Want to do another one?" I asked.

"Absolutely!"

We walked slowly back to the car below. The real fun of interval workouts is that everything is broken up between moments of intense activity and lengthy rest periods. During the rest period you can talk, make jokes, or simply enjoy the day. It took us about nine minutes to walk down to the bottom of the hill where we turned around and sprinted to the top again.

The second interval went better. I picked a pace I was able to sustain all the way to the top and finished the hill in under six minutes.

William came trotting up a few minutes later. He reached forward for the water bottles that we had left near the designated starting point and took a long drink.

"You know," he said suddenly, "sometimes I really wish that I'd been born with the genetics to be a great athlete."

I, too, took a drink and I looked at William sideways.

"You don't have good genetics?" I asked somewhat skeptically. "How do you know? Have you undergone some sort of fancy genetic testing or something?"

He seemed a little surprised at the question.

"Well, no, but I'm having a hard time running up this hill, aren't I?"

I shrugged, "Me too, but I don't think I'm having difficulty because genetics. I think I'm having a hard time because it's a big hill and we need to spend some more time training on it."

I turned to start walking down the hill again in preparation of our next interval. William came along, still thoughtful on the genetics topic.

"Don't you think some people are genetically better athletes than others?"

"Maybe," I said. "But there's nothing you can do about your genetics, so there's no point in even thinking about them. Instead of worrying about something you can't control, I think you should focus on doing everything you can to reach your full potential. Don't let yourself be discouraged by thinking the ceiling is lower for you than it is for anyone else. If you train like an Olympian, I think you might be surprised as to how good you get."

William was reflective as we did a couple more intervals before eventually heading home.

Throughout the next couple months, we'd head out every Wednesday to the Elk Mound Observatory to do our hill bounding interval workout. Every week we tried to do at least one more interval than the week before. The workout absolutely killed our legs, but it was immensely satisfying, and bit by bit we found ourselves getting much, much better.

After we'd been at it for about two months, we were both consistently running the hill around ten times in under five and a half minutes. In light of our improvement, William came over to me with a sincere expression on his face. Our training had trimmed him up considerably and added quite a bit of tone to his musculature. He was feeling a lot better about his prospects for the upcoming Birkie.

"Thanks for setting me straight about genetics," he said. "I guess I was kind of using that as an excuse."

I laughed. "Yes, it's always good to be discerning about common-knowledge beliefs that don't play out in your favor. When it comes to choosing genetics or hard work, I'll choose hard work every time. Don't ever listen to anyone who tells you there's a limit as to how good you can be."

CHAPTER 35

The years continued on and the Birkies came and went. My best race came the year the event ended at Highway OO because of a lack of snow. I finished 232nd, and although I was happy with the result, I felt I could have climbed higher up the result board if we had skied the complete distance. My goal had been to get into the top two hundred so I could consider myself an "elite" skier, or at least call myself one for a year.

Even though that didn't happen, I still had the thrill of sprinting out from the front line of the first wave and finding myself alone on the trail at the head of the great, multicolored, scaly beast that is the American Birkebeiner. On that day, I even managed to catch up with some of the elite women who had started a few minutes ahead. The trail was so fast that I hardly heard the jeers of the drunken snowmobilers as I flew by.

Oddly, the faster you become, the quieter and more soothing the race is. There's an odd calm at the front, the quiet before the storm. You're skiing by yourself between the first wave and the elite wave. Everybody behind you is trying to catch you, but when you know that they can't, there's nothing to be worried about.

That year was pretty much the highlight for me as a skier because I got sick shortly thereafter.

It was one of those weird sicknesses that lingered and lingered and lingered and was a total mystery to everybody.

I went to one hospital after another. The doctors poked and prodded me for ceaseless hours. The only reprieve came during the moments when the doctors gathered together in silence to discuss new and exotic areas to explore. The delight with which they broke huddle to set about the application of their trade led me to become suspicious of their motivations. When they ran out of poking and prodding ideas, they'd scamper out of the room, presumably to glean new inspiration from the consultation of ancient tomes of medieval torture techniques.

When they had poked and prodded everything, the real torture began.

Meanwhile, I was losing weight and although I was still trying to run and bike and ski like always, I just wasn't getting the job done.

Eventually, I went in and they had me drink a cup of liquid chalk before having a look at my abdomen on some fifty-thousand dollar machine.

"A-ha!" somebody said finally.

I relaxed thinking that perhaps they were done looking and I wouldn't have to surrender my last little shred of dignity after all.

Their conclusion was that my gall bladder was diseased.

"You're an odd candidate to have a bad gall bladder," my doctor said.

"Why?"

"Well," he continued, "for gall bladder disease we usually look for a person who embodies the three Fs."

"The three Fs?" I asked.

"Fat, female and fifty,'" he smiled. His smile disappeared as it dawned on him that he had just given away another doctor secret that might someday find its way into a book or something and embarrass the whole medical community. "Er … " he said, trying to bury the mistake, "you're obviously none of those … but the gall bladder is no good, so we should take it out."

"Take it out?"

"Yep."

"OK."

They took me in and gave me a bunch of injections and then wheeled me into an operating room. I vaguely remember laying deliriously on the stretcher telling everyone what a great job they were doing, because I wanted them to like me as they cut me open. Then I faded into nothing.

For those of you who don't know, when you go under anesthesia, there's nothing.

You don't dream.

You don't think.

Time doesn't pass.

The only thing that does happen, if you're lucky, is that you'll eventually hear somebody calling to you like you're at the bottom of a deep well. At first you won't want to go anywhere near the voice, but it keeps nagging at you until you're wearily roused, which is followed by an acceleration back into consciousness.

"Did you get it out?" I asked.

"Yup," they said.

And that was the end of my gall bladder. It's probably sitting on a desk at some medical institute somewhere.

***

Me sans gall bladder was better than I had been in the recent past, but not quite as good as I had been in the slightly more distant past. I tried getting into my training routine again, but it felt like I had been knocked down a couple rungs and I just didn't feel like traversing the same landscape all over again. Other shores were calling me … other lives.

So I buckled down and took interim and summer classes and finished my degree in a rush. I had been considering getting a master's degree in English, and most master's programs required a certain competency in at least one foreign language. Bearing that in mind, I figured I'd learn Spanish more quickly and efficiently by spending time in a

Spanish-speaking country than by wasting my life in another odious regimented classroom, so I jumped on a plane to Peru and made the ten-hour trip to the land of the Incas.

It ended up being a rather momentous decision.

Based on that choice, I ended up staying in Peru for nearly ten years and had a series of adventures that are beyond the scope of what I can get into here.

But Birkie fever never died in me, it just transformed.

I was an eternal traveler.

The Birkie had started all that, it had got me rolling, given me momentum, and launched me the moment I achieved escape velocity.

From Twin Pines, Wisconsin, to Melbourne, Australia, to Oberammergau, Germany, to Lima, Peru, the world called me and I glided from place to place.

These are the types of things you can do if you're willing, dedicated, and silly enough.

It's what the Birkie teaches you.

It's Birkie fever; it makes you do wild and wonderful things.

CHAPTER 36

After about a ten-year hiatus in Peru, I decided to do Grandma's marathon again. I made the arrangements to come back to the U.S. from Lima and met up with Dean Franklin. By then, Dean had become fairly well known in the skiing community. He was still a tremendous athlete and loved to participate in all the local events. He'd also spent time as a wax technician for the U.S. Ski team.

He recounted a story from some other event where he had been elected the U.S. guide and chaperone for Norwegian skier and multiple-gold-medalist Thomas Alsgaard.

"Yeah," Dean said in his enthusiastic way, "my boss came up to me and said, 'There's Thomas Alsgaard, go ski with him all day and never let him out of your sight!' Here's a guy that NOBODY ON THE PLANET can ski with all day … yet MY job is to 'not let him get out of my sight!'"

"What'd you do?"

"I said, 'To heck with that! *You* go ski with him and

don't let him out of your sight!'" he laughed. "No, I went skiing with him. It was good training, obviously." He said it humbly, but being able to ski with Thomas Alsgaard, even at a training pace, takes a pretty serious level of fitness.

We did a couple training runs and races to finish my preparation for Grandma's, and as the days of the event clicked by, I got more and more nervous.

But it was a good kind of nervous … that old familiar sense of nervousness from a decade before when my world was smaller and all I had to think about was skiing.

It was Dean's dad Neal who had been encouraging me to do Grandma's again. As the fateful day approached, he picked me up and drove us up to Duluth so we could crash for the night nearer to the race start and not have to make a two-hour morning drive.

There, on the verge of what was sure to be another momentous day of pain, I couldn't help but laugh reflectively at the crazy stuff I always got myself into.

The profound silliness that is involved with running 26.2 miles cannot be overstated. Some of us just don't have those willowy runner's bodies that are most effective for such an endeavor and we end up suffering every year because of it. Back when I was eighteen, I was about one hundred sixty-five pounds, but years of working as a restaurant critic, among other things, in Peru had caused me to grow into more of a King Leonidas-shaped two hundred-plus—do an Internet search for "300 Spartans" if you don't know who I'm talking about. The main difference between me and those ancient, ripped Greek warriors is that, while they had many little abdominal muscles bursting out all over the place, I had just one big one that drooped down in front.

My troubles began the night before the race. Instead of renting an expensive hotel or dorm room, Neal and I decided to go camping at a cost of ten dollars for two people. Not one to underestimate the value of a good night's sleep, I had brought the mattress from my bed along instead of some stupid, inflatable cushion. Well, it was nice and comfortable for most of the night ... and then the rain came.

As the water pooled beneath my tent, I couldn't help but notice that the sections of the foam mattress that had been most compressed by my weight tended to soak through.

Desperately, I tried to distribute my weight evenly across the mattress so that, though the bottom was wet, the top would remain dry.

This tactic was only minimally effective since I kept drifting off to sleep and rolling over only to shoot back to full alertness as half my body got drenched by the mattress beneath me, which had pretty much been converted to little more than a wet sponge.

I resorted to huddling on a damp corner of the foam while praying futilely for the sun to come with its warming rays. There is no greater teacher than experience, and I now understand the value of having an impermeable air mattress beneath me while camping.

But you always have a poor night's sleep before a marathon, so I was able to brush off that little misadventure with a hearty chuckle.

Neal awoke more refreshed than I was, but as we rode the bus to the starting line, he still had his concerns. He had been having some knee problems and hadn't run for more than forty minutes at a time in about two months, but his complete lack of training wasn't going to stop him. I hadn't trained enough either, and I knew it, but I didn't really feel like talking about it right then. Instead, we spent our pre-race hours trying to mentally work out a kind of hand-held harness that would allow you to run on all fours like a dog.

We figured this would make running a marathon a whole lot easier.

"Imagine if you waltzed up to the starting line next to all those Olympic hopefuls with some huge harness clasped to your arms that extended to the ground like the long limbs of a giraffe or something." Neal said.

"Boy, I bet you'd get some strange looks."

"They'd have to have rubber tips I guess, for traction."

"Heck yeah, and they'd have to be spring-loaded, and retractable for the back swing."

"I wonder how much faster you could go if you ran like a dog?"

"Or a horse."

"Yeah, a horse, what do you think?"

"Oh, heck, you'd do the whole marathon in 1:30 easy."

"1:30, you think so?"

"Oh yeah, no problem."

"But wouldn't you be disqualified?"

"Well they didn't disqualify Bill Koch for skate-skiing in the Olympics, did they? They didn't disqualify Greg LeMond for being the first to use aero bars, did they? The innovator always gets a free year."

"Hey, yeah!"

We daydreamed about it for a few minutes, basking in the glory of our imminent Grandma's victory and the money we were going to make with our patents. Suddenly I had a bad thought.

"Uh, Neal … "

"Yeah?"

"Aren't dogs' and horses' knees on backwards?"

He thought about it for a moment.

"Yeah, I think they are."

"So it wouldn't work to just extend our arms to the ground would it?"

"No, I guess we'd need some massive surgery."

"Massive surgery to switch your knees around?"

"Yeah ... "

Somehow that didn't seem to be worth the bother, but by then the race was about to start so we didn't have long to dwell on our lost fortune.

We didn't even hear a starting gun, but the crowd

surged forward, so we assumed the race was on. It started as a slow walk, but pretty soon people were breaking into an easy jog. Neal started to jog along with them.

"Hey Neal, what are you jogging for?" I said, noticing we hadn't crossed the timing sensor. "We aren't being timed yet!"

"Oh, yeah."

We walked leisurely the rest of the way to the starting line and then started running at the beep of our timing chip. Having been out of the training routine for a decade, I felt no pressure to perform well and that put me at ease. Our plan was to stop and walk every mile for thirty seconds to a minute. Neal had read about this technique in some runner's magazine. Apparently it was supposed to dramatically reduce the agony you would feel at the end of the race—however, some agony at the end of a marathon is unavoidable.

The miles clicked off. The thirty-second walk thing seemed to be working. We were doing about eleven-minute miles, which was better than the fifteen I thought was the best I was capable of. Before the race, I'd been telling people I was going to run to the thirteen-mile marker and then just walk in.

Neal was doing great for basically not having trained at all. But just short of ten miles, he sent me off. It was a touching scene.

"I'm hurting, you're making me go too fast."

"Sorry, I can slow down."

"No, I can't help it, when I run with you, I start getting competitive. Go … save yourself … leave me."

"OK, cheers."

The minute I started running alone, I foolishly decided to pick up my pace for a couple miles while dreams of my youthful, sub-four-hour marathons flashed through my addled brain. At about mile nineteen, I started to pay for this burst of enthusiasm. My pace dropped to the fifteen-minute-mile mark I had been dreading.

It started to not be such fun. My knees hurt, my quads burned, my breathing was labored, and I realized something crazy would have to be done for me to even finish.

Desperate measures were required.

At about mile twenty, a couple college frat boys were standing by the side of the road drinking beer and egging on the runners as much as rooting for them.

"Come on man, you know you're liking it!" One of them said, catching my eye.

"Hey, why don't you give me a beer!" I snapped back.

The guy paused like he didn't know if I was serious.

"I *am* serious!" I cried. "I'm *dead* serious! Give me a *beer*!" I reached forward with the empty water cup I had unknowingly been clutching for the last mile or two.

"Nobody sees this," he cautioned as he filled up my glass from his can making furtive looks in all directions. I'm not really sure what he was worried about, but after living in Peru for a decade, I was an expert in smuggling contraband (just kidding, DEA), and the transaction was made without interruption.

I ran six steps, slammed the beer, and suddenly the marathon changed completely. It was as if little cartoon characters had been drawn along the course. They reared up in the air on cute little hind legs and cheered with tittering abandon.

Suddenly, I felt great!

"Beer power!" I cried and jumped forward with a jolt of energy. Almost instantly, I was back to an eleven-minute pace, the miles clicked by. The tiny shot of alcohol relaxed my weary muscles. The carbohydrates and calories of the beer filled me with mystical force.

"Beer is a sports beverage!" I said to myself. Why hadn't I ever realized this before?

At about mile twenty-one, I found another frat boy and this one tossed me an entire can. The next four miles were a glorious blur as I jogged along, occasionally lifting the frothing vessel of amber joy to my face.

"Hey, that guy's got a beer," came the admiring shouts from the crowd, inevitably followed by a swelling roar of applause.

"There's a sandwich in every can!" I called, holding the beer up like a trophy.

"Come back here when you finish and we'll buy you some more!"

The spectators loved me. Here was a marathoner they could identify with. Even though I was out there doing something they'd never dream of doing, I shared a common love, the love of beer. There I was in the flesh, the missing link between couch potato and elite athlete, an ambassador to the non-runners of society.

The beer-guzzling marathoner!

A folk hero, just like Johnny Appleseed.

"I love this guy!" somebody yelled.

"I love you too, man!"

I don't know what sports nutritionists would attribute it to, but nobody passed me for the rest of the race.

Coming up to the final mile, I glanced down at my watch and noticed I had about twelve minutes to finish to get in under five hours. I wanted to ignore it, to just put my head down and trot. But I couldn't. Those old competitive juices started flowing. And everybody knows that 4:59 looks much better than 5:01 on the results list.

I was going good, but there was still so far to go. At mile twenty-six I had 1.5 minutes in the bank.

Two-tenths of a mile to go.

It was going to be tight.

Should I sprint?

Would the beer come back and bite me in the butt?

Would I pass out?

I sprinted.

The seconds ticked away.

1:10

1:05

1:00

The banner didn't seem to be getting any closer.

At thirty seconds, I was pretty sure I wasn't going to make it.

At fifteen seconds, I toyed with the idea of taking off my shoe with the timing chip and throwing it across the line, NFL-style ahead of me—would that count? Sure it would, I was the innovator … I'd get a free pass.

In the end, I just sucked it up and finished.

Chip time 5:00:17.

A personal record for me at two hundred pounds. And maybe it's even a course record for two bills, too, since nobody bothers to keep track of such things, although it probably isn't. Seriously, when you think about it, they shouldn't award medals for age classes, they should award them for weight classes. I mean, they don't have boxing matches based on age do they? That would be absurd! Why is it any different with running and skiing marathons?

As I stood there gasping for air at the finish line, it occurred to me that an even better idea would be to have a handicapped marathon where every racer has to carry weights to make their load two hundred pounds. Heavier racers could be tied off with helium balloons or given time bonuses for every pound they were over.

Realizing what a silly idea that was, I wiped my brow and made my way to the beer tent, resolving to lose thirty pounds for next year. That plan seemed a lot easier to implement than the handicapped marathon idea.

I turned in my ticket for a free beer.

"Do you want regular or light?"

I looked at her sideways.

"On days that I run 26.2 miles, I feel I can allow myself a few indulgences."

She handed me the appropriate bottle.

It had been a good day.

CHAPTER 37

Soon after that, circumstances conspired to allow me to get back into my beloved Birkie.

In January 2009, I married my lovely Peruvian wife, and after battling with immigration authorities for about six months, we managed to get her a visa to come and live in the U.S.

In October 2009, we stepped off the airplane into the Minneapolis airport. Outside, it was a lovely fall day that my wife enjoyed greatly. As the weeks passed into a frigid December and January winter, my wife wasn't happy with the move. Wisconsin winters are an acquired taste—some say its appreciation isn't possible without first freezing off a significant number of brain cells or eliminating them in the method of your preference.

I took her to the various ski events of the region and, despite her aversion to the cold—they don't have snow in Lima, Peru—she couldn't help but be taken by the pageantry of the local races.

"We'll have to get you on skis! You might be the first Peruvian to ski the Birkie!"

The idea appealed to her.

Throughout the winter, the Birkie hovered on the horizon, waiting for us to come to it, rather than the other way around. It was like an old friend with an arriving airplane ticket for a distant day, and I was extremely anxious for the reunion.

The fever grew, and grew … and then the day arrived.

True Birkie fever had been threatening to make its presence felt for the last four or five months, but it didn't strike as a full-on, certifiable case until 4:30 on the morning of Saturday, February 27, 2010. I was staying at my mom's house in Twin Pines, Wisconsin, which is a convenient 30 minutes from Hayward, and I had just settled into that blissful half-hour of nervous sleep before the great event when there was a pounding on my door. I sighed. It was just like the old days.

"Get up! It's 4:30, we've got to get on the road!"

It was my mom, and after twenty-three previous Birkies I think the fever had come to stay.

"Mom, the buses don't even start until six and we're only a half-hour away."

But there was no reasoning with the fever.

"No, the way is riddled with perils! There's traffic and asteroids and aliens and moose! Flocks of them! They'll bite the wheels right off my truck!"

It wasn't worth fighting since I wasn't about to get back to sleep anyway, so I stumbled out of bed and slithered into the high-tech, ultra-wicking, technologically superior ski outfit that I'd carefully laid out the night before. This was to be my eighth Birkie, after nearly a decade of non-participation. Still, I knew what I was in for. I had even dragged a couple old tricks out of my foggy memory, such as putting your ski gloves and hat into your warm-up jacket pockets so there would be no chance of losing or forgetting them before the race start.

You see, Birkie fever does strange things to a person. It makes you susceptible to the most obvious and stupefying oversights. Even earlier that year, I'd seen a guy at the start of the pre-Birkie lining up with only one glove since the other had disappeared into feverland, and the pre-Birkie provokes only a *mild* case of fever. There are tales of people who have gotten up at four, made it to the buses, gotten dropped off at Telemark, and only then realized that they'd forgotten their skis.

It happens!

It's like that recurring dream about finding out on the last day of finals that you have a class on your schedule for which you failed to attend even one lecture—I still have that dream and I graduated eons ago.

So it was pretty much fear of the fever that got us up and rolling and out the door by five a.m. and into the pitch blackness of Birkie morning. As we rolled through Twin Pines, there was another burst of panic as we passed by the temperature display on the local bank.

"Oh my God! It's only eight degrees! I'm waxed for twenty-five! I'm done for!"

"Relax, the race doesn't start for four more hours. It's going to get warmer."

"Moose!"

I'm not even sure who cried out the last. But it turned out to be a false alarm. Our vehicle was filled with seven people, as it must be on Birkie morning, none of whom I'd met before. But we were united in our quest, so that made them family, I suppose.

As we rolled into the Cable parking lot, I was surprised to realize that we weren't even the first to arrive. In fact, of the seventy or so people on that six a.m. bus, about thirty were close personal friends who I'd skied with for years—it turns out, getting up at four-thirty a.m. is a pretty veteran move. Mel Wallace was there, William Cross, David, Ethan, Kathryn, Dean... and if I squinted my eyes, I could almost imagine that my Grandpa was the bus driver, cackling joyously about the prospect of showing us how not to drive on black ice.

"Hey!" they all cried euphorically.

"You made it!"

"Great to see you!"

"How did you avoid the moose?"

By the time we arrived at Telemark, there was light in the sky. We found a corner to hunker down in, left our stuff, and made our way to the bathroom lines. It's all about getting in line on Birkie morning. Even if you don't have to go when you initially take your place in line, chances are you'll have to by the time it's your turn.

The flow of people at the Telemark lodge in the wee hours before the Birkie is phenomenal. You see everybody.

Every single person who has ever been at any one of the ski trails that you've trained on that year is there. The guy you once saw wearing snowshoes and walking his dog is there. The guy dressed in blaze-orange carrying a rifle who nearly mistook you for a deer and blew your head off is there. Everybody who has ever put on a pair of skis, or even looked at a pair of skis in a store or catalog is hunkered down in some quiet corner of the Telemark lodge awaiting the start of their wave.

There is a gentle buzz. Time passes quickly and you spend most of it wondering if you, perhaps, can make it to the bathroom one last time—a risky proposition.

With about an hour to go before the start, we finally gathered our gear and headed out. At this point, you aren't even making your own decisions anymore. You're part of a vast collective, caught up in an irresistible current. The flow picks you up and carries you to the race start. Along the way, you bounce around other bodies like an errant pin ball. Things accelerate. Suddenly you start to question whether getting up at four-thirty had been early enough. Perhaps next year you should shoot for four? Or three-thirty? After all, what if there had been a moose?

With a half hour left to go, you're peeling off your warm-ups.

The warm-ups go into backpacks—bringing a backpack is another veteran move.

The backpacks go into the official Birkie gear bag with your race number scrawled on the side.

The gear bags go into a truck.

You trot to the start and … wait.

The very slowest time of year is the last ten minutes before your wave's start time at the Birkie.

You watch the skiers in the pen ahead of you, shuffling like cattle eager to begin their journey to the slaughterhouse. In addition to the nervousness and the endless mental checklists that you've been going through again and again and again, there's the second-guessing about the effect not trying to get to the bathroom one last time is going to have on your race.

And there's also the cold.

The adage goes that if you're not cold before the start, you're dressed too warm.

But there's little comfort in knowing you're dressed right when you're freezing your cheeks off.

The countdown begins.

Ten minutes …

Five …

One …

And finally you're off, scurrying down the tracks, double-poling like mad even though there's no point because you'll never be able to keep up that pace throughout the whole race. But everybody goes fast in the first hundred yards, if only to just get the blood back flowing through their frozen fingers.

I was in wave five, and like always, there were a couple

guys who took off like a shot the second the gun went off, never to be seen or heard from again. Those were the elite skiers who had been out of the mix for a while and were relegated to earning their placement in the lower waves. Once they're out of the way, things get oddly calm. You've made it! You're doing the race! You didn't forget anything and now you just have to wait patiently until Hayward arrives.

Starting the Birkie is an eerie calm.

You're back home. Back in the surreal world that only exists between a starting point and a finish line while under the influence of a running timer.

The course was still fast in the fifth wave, although the trail was pretty well ground up on most of the uphills. The downhills were fine on the straight sections, but curved downhills were littered with those infamous "Birkie ruts" that come from too much snowplowing. Birkie ruts are an interesting phenomenon that only develop in races with thousands of people. They are comprised of piles of powdery snow separated by planes of glare ice approximately two feet wide. You can use the snow piles to guide you down the hills by jamming one of your skis into the corner and just riding the edge of the pile, but if somebody wipes out in front of you, evasive maneuvers are problematic.

As I made my way through my eighth Birkie, a couple things stood out. There was the preacher and the nuns on Bitch Hill who forgave our sins of screaming profanity as we climbed that infamous final obstacle. There was a guy quietly skiing along with a bib proclaiming he'd skied thirty-five Birkies—I believe there had only been thirty-seven at the time. It seemed kind of a shame that this guy would be skiing in relative anonymity. Sure, he got a pale yellow bib, but that's a far cry from the red bibs of the founders and the honor of starting before the elite wave. I think they should have a neo-founder category for those who have completed thirty-five plus Birkies so that they can rotate a couple of these tremendous Birkie skiers into the limelight on occasion. Finally, I saw a guy hit a chipmunk that fell out of a tree. For a moment, I didn't realize what had happened and I thought he'd dropped his hat. It was only when I reached down to pick it up that I noticed it was writhing and twitching on the ski trail and that I was better off swerving to avoid it since it wasn't the type of thing anybody would want handed to them.

"That's a new one," somebody said.

"At least it wasn't a moose."

On Lake Hayward, they were offering shots of Jagermeister and Jim Beam. At that point, I was still hoping to finish in under 3:40, so I made the incorrect decision of not partaking. I finished in 3:41.

At the finish, a slew of people were there to help skiers with things like taking off skis, handing out warm clothing, bowls of soup and plastic cups of beer. It was one of those rare days when the trail was fast and the temperature was warm so everyone finished happy and the party on Main Street became one of those mystical eternal moments.

Events like the American Birkebeiner are special

because it's there that life's lessons are learned. The fever may have temporarily ebbed in me, but it never abated, and in three hundred sixty-plus days, I, along with thousands of other Birkie faithful, would once again be smacking an alarm clock at 4:30 a.m., worrying about my wax and endeavoring to avoid the moose.

It's best to be prepared … they might come out in force next year. I know the skiers will.

It was good to be back.

CHAPTER 38

B irkie fever!
It doesn't matter if you're old or young, thick or thin, fast or slow, it treats everyone the same.

People think of many things when they hear the words.

Some think of Prince Haakon being carried to safety.

Some think of Tony Wise.

Some think of Hayward, Wisconsin.

I think of the fun involved, the festivities, the traveling and the joy that exists in no other place than at the finish line of that magical event as thousands of people come together and celebrate the fact that they've all done something silly and magnificent and wonderful.

For a few weeks a year, the American Birkebeiner brings the world to Wisconsin.

And if you happen to be in Wisconsin during the Birkie month, this gathering might act as the catalyst to get you out of your comfort zone.

It's your ticket to new places.

New experiences.

New people.

Birkie fever!

It means something different to everybody, and beyond Birkie fever the whole wide world awaits.

Don't just sit there. Get some skis! Fill in an entry form! Join the party!

Find out what Birkie fever will mean for you.

As for me, I recently became a father and I'm dearly looking forward to the day when I take my seven-year- old daughter on her first mini-expedition through the corn fields. Surely there will come a moment when she feels it's too much, and she'll throw herself to the ground just like Daddy did when he was her age.

"Carry me," she'll say.

I suppose I could stoop down and lift her up in an all-enveloping hug. Giving my daughter hugs is right at the top of the list of things that I love to do most in this world. But hopefully I'll have the strength to share the same lesson that my mother shared with me when I was in that same position making that same demand.

It's a lesson that's far more valuable and far more empowering than a mere helping hand.

It's a lesson you can find solace in during all of life's inevitable highs and lows.

Having someone there to carry you is nice.

Cross-country skiing, however, teaches you how to carry yourself.

The End

Walter Rhein was born in northern Wisconsin. As he grew up, he developed a deep appreciation for cross-country skiing, the American Birkebeiner, and the Worldloppet circuit. His pursuit of international cross-country ski races sparked a powerful wanderlust that resulted in a ten year period spent living and working in South America. However, a true skier cannot resist the call of winter forever, and Rhein has recently relocated to Wisconsin, at least for the time being. He currently contributes articles to the run, bike and ski blog at CyclovaXC.com, and produces fantasy novels for Rhemalda Publishing. Feel free to contact him for questions or interviews at walterrhein@gmail.com, and be sure to check out his personal website at www.LetItRhein.com and his blog at www.swordreaver.com.

CPSIA information can be obtained
at www.ICGtesting.com
Printed in the USA
LVHW011556170119
604290LV00017B/588

9 781492 879343